Lennon Steps

Petra Monaco

Other Books by Petra

Betrayal: The Journey – Childhood memories and the Adult awakening

Lennon Steps

By Petra Monaco

ISBN-10:1507588798
ISBN-13: 978-1507588796

Copyright © 2015 Petra Monaco
Printed in the United States of America

Notice of Rights
All rights reserved. No part of this book may be reproduced or transmitted in any from by any means, electronic, mechanical, photocopy, recording or other without the prior permission of the publisher.

For information on getting permission for reprints and excerpts, contact petra@fosteredlife.com

Notice of Liability
The author is sharing a personal story and no part of this story shall be used for diagnosis. Not every genetic disorder or organ transplant is the same and everyone's journey is different. The Author has omitted some names and changed but all accounts of the story are accurate to the authors memory and entries in a blog.

DEDICATION

This book is dedicated to everyone that was touched by Lennon in some way. It is dedicated to you because you supported, prayed, rallied behind Lennon during the darker days and the lighter days.

It is dedicated to everyone who is an organ donor, the families who have made the decisions for their loved ones to be organ donors, and the three families that have touched our lives in ways we could never imagine.

ACKNOWLEDGMENTS

Many people helped me directly in the editing stages of the book you hold in your hands. It is my heartfelt thanks to Lydia who has taken time on Sunday mornings to has out the scenes and Kevin who reviewed time and again. I want to thank the amazing women who have supported me in this with encouragement and support from near and far.
Thank you for my kids who continue to show me how amazing they are!

Part One

Four months pregnant, I was standing behind the counter making a pizza order for a customer. I tossed the dough into a round shape and added the sauce, cheese and toppings. I was nauseous and feeling ill, trying to not vomit all over the counter. I was miserable. I hadn't told anyone I was pregnant up to this point. I had waited to share the news because I had several miscarriages before and just needed to feel sure that I was not going to lose another baby.

While I was filling the bins with sausage, pepperoni, and cut the tomatoes, a conversation with my co-worker pissed me off. I spilled the news to my co-workers in a hormonal surge. I could no longer hide my growing belly nor the morning sickness; I was experiencing as I continued to run to the bathroom chatting with the porcelain god about how I hated morning sickness.
It was January and I was moving into a 3-bedroom mobile home with my boys and their dad in Newport News, just outside of Tidewater, Virginia. It was the

perfect location for the kids' dad, Joey, because it was 2 minutes away from the pizza place that he managed. Joey could cover my shifts when I was too ill to work. I am one of those people who carries their own weight and try not to let anyone down, but this pregnancy wore me down.

Kevin, my oldest son, had the genes of my German father, tall and skinny boy and his blue eyes too. Kevin was in 4th grade and struggled with school. Well, he didn't just struggle he hated school. I agonized to get him to do his homework. He would play when he should be doing homework or cleaning or even sleeping. Kevin diagnosed with Attention Deficit Disorder a few years back after a miserable year in kindergarten.

In hindsight, with three kids under my belt, I know that a child's experience of the first year of school dictates whether he will love or hate it for years to come. Kevin loathed doing any kind of work for school but went. He still managed to pass all his tests. When you asked him what he likes about school, he would tell you that math is his favorite, but would rather play video games. Kevin -- a smart kiddo, that one, although frustrating.

Kevin settled into the new home and made friends quickly with a neighbor girl close to his age, Shelby. It was his excuse to get away from his younger brother Jarod, with whom he shared a room.

Jarod was nothing like his older brother: born with red hair, he was funny and sensitive. At the age of 5, he was young enough to still have imaginary friends. One time, his dad started to sit down on the couch, when Jarod yelled at him to not sit there. His dad jumped back up in confusion. Jarod was so upset that his dad sat on his friend. I ended up on the floor laughing with tears streaming down my face.

Jarod did soon make a real friend, the younger sister of Kevin's new friend. The two girls and their family became close friends with our family. The girls' mom, Michelle, was born in Germany, and her mom still spoke with a thick accent. I missed home every time I spoke to them. I left Germany at 18 to move to the USA. Settling into the new place and working, the pregnancy began taking its toll on me. I usually love summer because it's celebrating Kevin's birthday and the warmth but not when pregnant. The closer I got to my due date the more eager and ready I was to have this baby, so that I could start feeling normal again.

I was ready to handle the challenge of raising another boy. The boys were easy - although I had no comparison.

Boys are what I knew.

Lennon decided he would be 5 days late. A hidden message that perhaps he does things his way?

The doctor induced me the morning of June 24th, 2003. Lennon sneezed his way into the world after only four hours of labor.

I didn't have maternity leave from the pizza place, but with their dad pulled double duty to cover my shifts. I was able to stay home for about a month with Lennon. The older boys were on summer break and spent most of their day running around the trailer park.

We had only been home a few days from the hospital. I was home alone with Lennon, crocheting a blanket on the couch. Crocheting has been a passion of mine since I was 17 years old and pregnant with my oldest, Kevin. Lennon was laying on the floor on his Elmo blanket, a chubby baby with only a little white fuzz on his bald head. We were watching "The Wiggles," one of those obnoxious children's shows with songs that we parents endure for the sake of our kids - "Yummy, Yummy Fruit Salad" is still stuck in my head twelve years later. With Kevin, it was Barney the Purple Dinosaur, while Jarod obsessed over the Teletubbies. In all honesty, I would rather listen to The Wiggles than watch Teletubbies any day!

I sang along with the songs and hoped to make them fun for Lennon, stepping out of my own comfort zone to try to engage him with the music.

In the middle of my next stitch, Lennon began to cry. I picked him up and offered him a bottle, but he spit it right back out. I changed his diaper even though it was not dirty. He continued to cry. I held him, rocking him back and forth, and he was still crying. I placed him in his stroller and walked around the block - the crying continued.

I find my calm when listening to music or crocheting. I wondered what his calm would be? I read psychology books as my hidden passion and remembered that not everything works for everyone. Sometimes you should try things out until you find what works. He appeared to like "The Wiggles" when they were on the television, but this time that wasn't enough. Maybe water could work? I decided to give him a bath. Call it intuition.

The boys' bathroom was at the end of the hall. I drew a bath in the white tub covered with a fish shower curtain, checking the temperature. The second I placed him into the water; Lennon stopped crying. He cooed lying in his tub seat for 45 minutes -- so long the water was almost cold.

I took him out of the tub and wrapped him in his towel, and he immediately began to cry. So, we repeated the ritual. Lennon attached to my hip, in every way. I'd sit on the edge of the tub, holding him, checking the temperature of the water and placed him back in the tub seat. I had learned that water was his reprieve during those hours of crying. It seemed he comforted, perhaps reminiscing still being in utero? Protected from something, although I had no idea what.

Lennon needed me to console and no matter what I tried nothing would satisfy him. He constantly had a runny nose and without any real explanation he would just scream for weeks on end.

It was difficult to do the l tasks one must do to keep a family going, like grocery shopping because the instant Lennon was in the car he would cry. He would scream while I pushed I pushed the cart. It was hard being in public when your child is crying and screaming and nothing works to comfort him. The stares of judgment covering every inch of you, and you wondered what they were thinking? Why can't she quiet the baby? What a bad mom she must be?

The Andrea Yates trial was still fresh in my mind - the mother who drowned her 5 children. I could feel compassion for her. I was at a loss on how to quiet my own child and nearing perhaps my own break. I was feeling like a failure as a mom. I never ever had a plan, but did sometimes wonder if death was the only option. We were in the living room. I had tried everything to console Lennon. Nothing worked. I laid him on his blanket on the floor and began sobbing on my knees, looking at him helplessly.

It was agonizing trying to comfort him, and it almost became too much to bear. I reached out to my friend Michelle. Without her assistance, I was not sure how much longer I could hold on.

Michelle lived three doors down from us and would take Lennon for a few hours. I would sit at home, smoking a cigarette to catch my breath.

There were many moments when Michelle and I took turns driving the car, cradling Lennon, giving him a bath or walking him in the stroller - but to no avail.
I called the doctor explaining the symptoms of screaming. He would recite that it's colic and not much else.

But other times, Lennon would sleep for hours and what felt like days. I had to wake him to make sure he was alive and breathing. This brought on different challenges, as sometimes he was difficult to walk. I would wonder why he was so tired, but chalked his sleeping off him being a good baby.

After a month of being home, I went back to work. It was time for their dad to handle the day, while I parented in the evening.

I was back at work for 2 hours when their dad called me

and told me I am fired from the pizza shop. He fired me from work because he couldn't handle staying at home with Lennon. The screaming and crying was too much.

***

Lennon grew.

His crying turned to vomiting. Naps, which babies have to have, became constant drowsiness -- after breakfast, during playtime. There was little playing or smiling. His symptoms seemed like the flu, but he had neither a fever nor a cough. Lennon was miserable.

When he wasn't sleeping, Lennon was manic and hyper. He ran around - go, go, go. I was glad he was an early walker, like his older brother Jarod. But that meant he could act on his restless impulses -- unable to sit long enough to eat his meals. His other brother, Kevin, diagnosed with ADHD, but Lennon's actions looked more severe.

Even at the age of one, their kids have a fear. But Lennon didn't. He was jumping off the couch without worrying about risk. He got into the pool without being able to swim. If he thought of it - he did it.
I was grateful that Kevin and Jarod loved to spend the days outside rather than in the house. It was challenging enough to care for Lennon and still meet the needs of the boys. I tried to be the perfect 1950's housewife and

mother. I often found myself just saying yes to whatever the boys asked. I felt such relief that for a moment that they did not need my attention that I often forgot to ask where they were going.

I was no longer sure how I was keeping it all together, finding myself in tears most of the time. I always knew something was wrong with Lennon -- something didn't feel right in my gut. One day, Lennon was really out of it, so Joey I decided to take him to the emergency room. When we arrived, no one immediately responded to our needs. All of a sudden, one of the emergency room techs noticed that Lennon should probably needed to receive fluids intravenously. The doctors evaluated, ordered lab work and came back with the diagnosis of dehydration. They continued fluids. Once Lennon was responsive, they sent us home.

During another emergency room visit two weeks later, they suspected that he had pneumonia and treated him with medication and sent us home with a list of what to do.

Despite these concerns, Lennon was meeting most developmental milestones, including crawling and walking. As he neared the age of two, I noticed his speech was not developing the way the other two boys did. I wondered this should be a concern, knowing that children do develop differently. It was frustrating because I was unable to decipher what he needed. Was he hungry? Was he thirsty? I couldn't tell.

I noticed that his independent play was virtually non-existent. He had cars and dinosaurs but would just stare at them looking absolutely lost on what to do with them. Other clues I barely noticed because I thought they were normal, like the delayed potty training. Lennon's older brothers took their sweet time, so I wasn't really surprised that Lennon was not quite ready to make the leap from diaper to toilet. I would place him on the potty and he would stare.

He just stared with no facial expressions. His smiles were elusive, his anger expressed through screaming.
It frustrated me that he couldn't find the independence that most 2 year olds would start to express. You know, the kind that pulls on your heartstrings, about how fast they are growing but then so proud as they become their own little person.

When Lennon was two months shy of being three years old, he still did not have a vocabulary. I contacted the school for an evaluation, and they determined he was significantly delayed by 1-2 years. My heart sank.
All we ever wish for as parents is to have healthy children. It's blindsiding when we learn that something is wrong with them.

At the same time, perhaps I was receiving my answer. Perhaps his speech delay was the doorway to the discovery of what I felt in my gut - which something simply was off with Lennon. The school's recommendation was to enroll him in pre-kindergarten. It seemed that if it was not one thing, it was another.

Next, Lennon became aggressive. One afternoon, he started hitting me for no reason. I tried saying, "Don't hit me. Please stop," but he just kept going. I remember sitting in my living room floor, wrapping my arms around him like a hug to pin his arms down. I cried. Later, during a friend's visit, Lennon threw her tiny Yorkshire terrier. I was unable to explain his aggression, and he was unable to explain his frustration. These episodes would also occur at school. They recommended that Lennon see a psychologist, even at the young age of three.

The psychologist suggested that Lennon might be allergic to Red40, a common food dye that can make children aggressive. We removed all foods out of his diet that included Red40 and reported back what we noticed. Maybe it was an illusion, but I did think that cutting out all the dye made some difference. We had better days where he cried less, but he still hit.
When Lennon was asleep, I kept thinking what a good baby he was and almost forgot how difficult his waking moments were. The older Lennon got, the screaming and

crying lessened. But the sleeping for long periods of time continued, sometimes for 8 to 10 hours. I just told myself he liked to sleep a lot. Except for when he didn't.

No matter how much I tried to get a routine for Lennon and his sleep schedule, it just didn't happen. It became the norm that I was up with him till 1 or 2 in the morning trying to get him to go to sleep. When he did finally crash it would only last for four hours or so, or just an hour or two. And then there were the periods when he slept a lot and got sick a lot.

It was so challenging to judge day to day what each moment would be like. It just didn't make any sense at all.

With every doctor's visit or emergency room visit my faith, in the medical profession disappeared. I couldn't fathom that there was something seriously wrong with my child, but no one could figure it out. To make it worse, no one was listening to me.

Deep down I knew something was wrong and feared the worst for my son. Yet with each doctor's appointment I began wondering if I was just imagining things.
I started to question my skills as a mother.
Confirming intuition

And then I became a single mother, on top of it all. The boy's dad and I split up. He had an opportunity through the pizza shop to move to Richmond. And the boys and I didn't move with him.

I had to get a babysitter to watch the boys after school while I was at a new job with a temp agency. I finally got to use my accounting skills at a job as a bookkeeper, even a few months before I graduated with my bachelors' degree.

I drove the boys an hour and a half to Richmond to see their dad whenever got a break in his schedule at the pizza shop. But I was ready to move on from our relationship.

I met someone online, and we had been chatting back and forth. He was also a single dad, but lived three hours away. We met up when time allowed.

Finally, I decided to move in with him in January 2007, from urban Newport News to rural Scottsville, Virginia. Of course his name was Kevin, too, so we called him Big Kevin. To make room for him and his daughter, Katie, we moved from a three-bedroom mobile home that felt extremely small to a four-bedroom double wide home with lots of yard.
We spent time together playing soccer or baseball. Even Lennon tried to play with us.

Our dog Dakota, a Husky-Rottweiler mix loved running around in the fenced yard, like she just regained freedom.

I still commuted for a few months from Scottsville to Newport News for a job but soon realized that driving three hours each day twice a day was just a little bit insane. I started job searching and began working as a bookkeeper for a temp agency.

Life felt stable and appeared normal.

During the summer we made our slip-n-slide with trash bags and a garden hose. Family time was a priority when we weren't working, or the kids were at school or I was finishing up another homework assignment for my accounting degree.

At dinnertime, Lennon would not eat everything on his plate. He would eat the vegetables but not the meat. I didn't push the issue. I don't know why not.

The temp job ended and I began delivering papers from 2 a.m. until 6 a.m. The hours of the work were brutally early, but still ideal as my partner was working as a mechanic during the day. So, we could keep the kids at home, with income to still provide for Kevin, Jarod, Katie, and Lennon.
Lennon continued days of being extremely lethargic and vomiting. My instinct was to give Lennon Pedialyte every time he threw up, thinking he was losing some electrolytes. When Lennon did feel like eating, we would give him what he wanted because it is the only thing we

knew he would eat -- chips and French fries. We offered McDonald's, but he only wanted French fries. Why didn't he want to his chicken nuggets?

Part Two

I had never been to a county fair, although we have similar carnivals in Germany, without the animal competition and the juried arts & crafts section.

The children excited to see the animals and even Lennon, now 4, was off time petting the goats. He was pointing and chattering with the few words that he had learned. Lennon excitedly went on the dinosaur, but standing outside watching him, I saw his head start leaning forward. Quickly he went to just looking sad and depressed. I asked Big Kevin beside me, "Does he look ok?"

Big Kevin and I made the decision to go to the emergency room. This was my first time at a local hospital since the move from the coast. I was hoping that this time, just maybe we could figure out what was going on. Perhaps this time, someone would finally listen to his history and be willing to explore what my gut has been telling me.

We immediately connected with Dr. M, and for the first time she listened to the concerns I had carried with me for so long. She was gentle in her questions and open to hearing answers before moving on to the next question. Lennon's body posture indicated he was at ease with her as he slumped down and made eye contact with her.

Dr. M requested the nurses at Martha Jefferson Hospital to do the usual routine of hooking him to an IV and taking some blood sent off to the lab. She looked him over and asked me for his entire history since pregnancy. Was he full term? How has his development been? What have you experienced? I gave her a run down about the sleeping, aggression, vomiting and lethargy. It was a little overwhelming.

Working with a new pediatrician like Dr. M felt like a second chance to find answers.

She reviewed the labs and noted that some of Lennon's amino acids did not appear quite right. She wasn't able to diagnose a problem, but wanted to watch him overnight. The nurses, once again, gave him fluids by IV in case of dehydration.

Lennon didn't like the IVs, though I'm not sure anyone would. But he was hungry. He asked for French fries. The nurses ordered pudding and fries. He's a slow eater; he hadn't even finished it all before he threw up.

The following day, Lennon was back to his normal self, chatting up a storm with words only he would know, smiling, holding his stuffed cat that his dad and I purchased when he was 3 months old.

Dr. M didn't find any cause for his symptoms, so she released Lennon from the hospital.

We went home and got ready for the first day of school for the year. Lennon would be in pre-kindergarten combined with special education for speech, occupational therapy and physical therapy.

Lennon got on the bus at 7:00 in the morning. It only took two hours, and the school called me to pick him up because something was seriously wrong.

I called Dr. M and took Lennon in, and, while on the drive to town that was 45 minutes away, Lennon began to vomit. His speech was incoherent - he was in and out of sleep and seemed delirious. It was like a drunken person - he would doze off and then pop awake and babble and doze off again.

At the pediatrician's office, we saw Dr. M in an examining room, but then had to wait for a while. I don't know why we had to wait. But Lennon was jumping off the examining table - over and over. He tried running out the door. Lennon hit me and he hit the nurses.

Embarrassed, I could do nothing.

Dr. M came back and told me to take Lennon to the other

local hospital, the University of Virginia Medical Center. UVA is a research and teaching hospital with all the best specialists in the area. I was hoping that I may now get some answers, scared what they might be.
But I didn't have time to feel scared - no phone calls to friends or even the thought to get myself dinner on the way to UVA. I just went from point A to point B on autopilot.

Once again, we found ourselves in an emergency room with an IV and blood tests. I recapped everything that I had experienced since his birth. Four years of endless nights of not sleeping, the days of sleeping, the continued vomiting and the speech delays and Lennon's lack of independence - at four he still wouldn't potty train.

The UVA Emergency Room doctor admitted Lennon to the hospital. I slept the night in a crappy old blue chair. In the morning, a genetics doctor arrived named Dr. W. I immediately panicked a little - oh my god, I must have fucked up DNA. But my other two boys are fine?

Lennon was playing with his stuffed cat and a few Matchbox cars.

Dr. W told me that Lennon's liver is missing an enzyme that processes the proteins we eat. Without that enzyme, your body produces too much ammonia, which can make you sick and vomit or lethargic.

Good grief, that's what we're living.

Too much ammonia, Dr. W said, can cause brain damage, coma or death. Normal levels of ammonia in our system are 30-60. Lennon's ammonia level was in the 450s.

What did the doctor just tell me? The information was still so unclear.

The diagnosis: Urea Cycle Disorder – Unspecified Dr. W suspected that, at times, since birth, Lennon's ammonia levels might have spiked much higher than 450. He made it clear that Lennon needed treatment, or he would die.

Urea Cycle Disorder is a rare metabolic genetic disorder, so Dr. W wanted to know if anyone else in our family had this disorder. I had no idea of knowing if this was in our family tree. I grew up in a foster home and had no connection to my family. I also didn't know if this ran on his father's side.

Scared, but relieved because I was finally validated. I had always known in my gut that something was wrong. That no other doctor had warned me just how bad this could have ended. Lennon could have died while we were waiting for answers.

I believe that if you put a request out to the universe, it

will help you find the answer. I met Big Kevin and moved to the area of this hospital at the exact moment we needed to learn about this rare genetic disorder. I believe things do happen for a reason, because we are always learning. I wondered what was it that I needed to learn? What did my son need to learn? What did my family need to learn? Or so it was something much bigger? Life took on a whole new meaning to me that day.

The doctors did not wait to act.

They transferred Lennon to the Pediatric Intensive Care Unit and placed him on intravenous medication to bring down his ammonia levels. But Lennon had lived for four years with all this ammonia in his system. His body reacted violently to the IV medicine as it started causing chemical changes. He became so angry, as if a demon had possessed him. He bit me on my shoulder as the nurse was trying to help give his medication. He leaped out of the bed as if he were to attack the nurse.

Lennon spent five days in the PICU until his ammonia levels were below 100, which Dr. W designated as Lennon's safe zone.

Staying in the safe zone was going to be hard.
Before the release from UVA hospital, Big Kevin and I had to learn Lennon's new routine.

Medication at 8 a.m., medication at 2 p.m. medication at

8 pm.

Amino Acid formula mixed with chocolate syrup, two or three times a day.

Only 10-15 grams of protein each day. (About two hard-boiled eggs - that's it.) No milk. No meat.

And constantly monitoring for symptoms of elevated ammonia:
- Loss of appetite
- Repeated vomiting
- Abnormal drowsiness
- Aggression
- Difficulty falling or staying asleep
- Falling asleep at inappropriate times
- Excessive total sleep time
- Delusions
- Hallucinations or even psychosis

On the day of discharge from the hospital, the wagon provided by the nurses loaded like a pack mule with several cases of formula, a supply of medication for 30 days, as well as toys collected during our stay. We headed home.

We arrived home and unpacked the car and piled the medication and paperwork on the dining room table. The routine of giving Lennon his medication began immediately. I crushed the big pills into a fine powder and masked the taste with applesauce.

Lennon's food schedule was not so rigid. The other kids, Jarod, little Kevin and Katie, all ate at the table at 6pm. Lennon sat there with us in his high chair, but he wasn't hungry. So, Big Kevin and I looked to four-year old Lennon to tell us when he was ready to eat. "Hungry" was a word in his limited vocabulary.

Together, Lennon and I sat on the floor and looked into the kitchen cabinet, staring at all my neatly organized lines of food. (I hate wasting time rifling through messy cabinets.) I reached in and picked up a can of cream of celery soup and asked Lennon, "Do you want this?" Lennon shook his head no. "Cream of mushroom soup?" and he nodded. I turned the can to read the label next: "Yay! It's zero protein!"

Even if the food had protein, like oatmeal, he is allowed to have some. We just had to keep track to make sure Lennon had no more or less than 10-15 grams a day. I now knew my son could die if he levels get out of hand. So I lived in a 24-hour crisis mode - always watching for signs and symptoms. You would think now that I had answers about Lennon's problems, I would be able to sit down and breathe. But there was no chance. I wasn't able to relax. I wondered if everything would be okay.

Doctors had missed Lennon's life threatening diagnosis

for four years. Frustrated that his previous doctors hadn't been curious enough to keep pushing for answers. But anger just wouldn't help. I naturally don't waste energy on feelings that don't serve me well.

Instead, the first night home from the hospital, I jumped into research to become more familiar with Urea Cycle Disorder: what is it? How much will the life, as we knew it change? Is my kid going to live? What if I mess up? What if I give him too much protein? What if I didn't give him his medication on time? What if the protein restriction or medication were not enough?

I went on a website recommended by the nutritionist for the UVA Medical Center's genetics department. She said there was a National Urea Cycle Foundation. It was a relief to know that my son, my family and myself were not alone as we learned about this disorder and how it would change our lives forever.

In people with Urea Cycle Disorder, the body breaks protein down only halfway, releasing too much poisonous ammonia in the blood and brain. My foster parents talked to me about protein as a kid - it was part of a balanced diet, part of the overall food pyramid. Now, years later as a mom, I found myself realizing I did not really know why protein mattered so much or how it affected the body.

A healthy body takes the protein we eat and breaks it into building blocks called amino acids. If excess amino acids are floating around, the body gets rid of them by changing them into ammonia. Ammonia is really toxic - gets broken down by several enzymes in the liver and changed into urea, which we pee out. This entire process is part of the urea cycle, and it occurs in liver cells.
The liver in a person with a urea cycle disorder is missing an enzyme necessary to convert ammonia into urea. As a result, ammonia, a highly toxic substance, builds up in the bloodstream and is not removed from the body. Untreated, the high amounts of ammonia can cause brain damage, coma and eventually death.

I know now why Lennon did not like Chicken Nuggets. He and his body instinctively knew what was or wasn't good for him.

Urea Cycle Disorder is so rare that only 1 in 8500 births have it. Some doctors suspect that UCD may be the hidden cause of some cases when an infant suddenly dies without reasons predicted by medical history, called Sudden Infant Death Syndrome or SIDS.
My mind needed to rest, but I was not sure that I could, but I went to bed that night grateful for finally having an answer.

***

The first morning home from the hospital, Lennon woke up disoriented. He was calling my name, looking for me, but we were both in the same living room. I watched him bumping into the corner of a desk.

I waved my hands above my head, saying, "I'm right here. Why can't you see me?" Confused - I know I'm short, but hey… He just kept calling my name. In his diaper and his cat in hand, he appeared to follow my voice.

"Can you see me, Lennon?"

"No"

I picked Lennon up, wondering, now what. Why did my son go blind within 24 hours? What else was going to happen?

I called Dr. W, the geneticist that had diagnosed Lennon barely a week before, trying not to sound hysterical. He recommended that we bring Lennon in and do a brain scan. I just grabbed Lennon's medicine and him and left. We went straight to the University of Virginia Medical Center's imaging department, where they saw us right away.

It took only a few hours to complete the tests, but felt like forever. Once again, Lennon was uncooperative and aggressive. He was hitting and kicking everyone in the room - nurses, doctors and me. I tried talking to him in a quiet voice, and he just screamed back at me. I'm pretty sure if he was older than four and could have said, "fuck you" or "shut up", he would have.

So, like they do for most kids, a nurse gave Lennon sedation medicine by IV in one arm while I held down the opposite arm. The team of nurses and doctors wrapped a bed sheet around him, kind of like a baby cocoon, to restrain him until he was calm.

The medicine kicked in and Lennon began his first of what would become many journeys down a tunnel-like machine that would scan his brain using magnetic resonance imaging, or MRI. This time, doctors were looking for possible causes of the blindness.

We hung out at the hospital waiting for the results. I was cuddling Lennon to provide us comfort while wondering what all of this meant. My brain was trying to make sense of it all to no avail. I knew however that I need to maintain composure for Lennon - my calm was is calm. Dr. W met us in the imaging waiting area with a serious face and I felt heaviness inside.

Lennon's brain scan showed more than 22 unnatural collections of fluid on the brain, called edemas. Several were directly behind and on the optic nerve impacting his vision.

Dr. W was clear that he was unable to drain the edemas

with surgery because of the risk involved. Devastated I sat there taking it all in.

The question -- why did this happen? Lennon managed to live through four years with undiagnosed Urea Cycle Disorder because his body adapted and found its own balance. Once diagnosed, the new medication drastically lowered ammonia levels in his body.

It was like a dam broke as his body started trying to flush out leftover ammonia that had build up over four years. The edemas were just one sign that his body was struggling to regulate its new chemical balance.
I asked Dr. W if Lennon would regain his eyesight. He wouldn't give a definite yes or no. I could feel that Dr. W was trying to give us hope but in reality he could not tell us the outcome we would love to hear.
Lennon's type of blindness was rare and uncommon, so Dr. W couldn't say for sure if it would be permanent or temporary. He was only aware of one other Urea Cycle Disorder-related blindness, and the boy stayed blind.

I'm a mother - I put myself in my son's shoes: Imagine being blind and you don't know if this is forever. Lennon's assistant teacher, Ms. Doe, called every day. "How are you, Petra?" I was ok. I had to be ok. I didn't have time to question how this would all turn out in the end. More importantly, though, I had a hard-earned abundance of strength to handle just about anything.

I was born to an alcoholic father. And then my foster dad drank, too.

I remember every night at dinner; my foster dad would have one to three or more beers or glasses of wine. In his angry moments, he would take his belt from his pants, chasing after me.

At eight, I set my mind to not be like my biological parents or my foster dad. Determined that if I were to have children I would love them and care for them and not overly criticize their every action.

As a teenager, I was drinking too much, just like him. My friends and I would get together after school in the gazebo beside the lawn of a historic castle in our town in Germany, Bad Homburg von der Hoehe. We drank bottles of Jack Daniels, Jägermeister, Jim Beam – whatever we could get our hands on. We smoked weed like it was going out of style.

But, unlike my dad and my foster dad, I quit. When I became pregnant at 17, I wanted to keep and raise my own kids to break the foster system cycle. I knew I could be the kind of mom my new baby needed me to be. Bailing out as a parent was never an option, not when little Kevin was born, not when I didn't know what was going on with Lennon and not now. The resilience within me knew that I would be able to handle this too, and that

Lennon somehow would be all right.

But these thoughts were not always easy. I contemplated "why me – why my kid" because frankly had I not been through enough already?

However, I also knew that focusing on those negative thoughts would not help keep my child alive. Every time a negative thought entered into my mind, I would turn it into a positive statement. Instead, I would ask myself what could I do, what is the best way to handle this situation. I had done this process for so many years that it was just natural.

I am a Libra and find that I have always balanced my options by looking at other people's perspectives. I needed to emphasize what Lennon was going through, because if I panicked about his blindness, then he would panic too. I needed to reassure him that everything would be all right, even if I were not 100% certain.

We spent another week in the hospital adjusting to his blindness, needing more guidance than before. The doctor referred us to the Virginia School for the Deaf and the Blind in Staunton, Virginia. The school assigned a vision specialist for Lennon, who would come to his public school to help Lennon maneuver through his school life. I was grateful that the vision specialist would come to see him at his local school and that we did not have to transport him. Any amount of stress and deviation from his routine could elevate Lennon's ammonia at any moment.

Lennon has an unwavering spirit that pushes him on and on, as if nothing and no one can keep him down. From September 2007 until January 2008, we were able to manage Lennon's urea cycle disorder on our own without hospitalization. We had regular checkups to watch his weight and manage his diet. Lennon was a forced vegetarian, but still ate what he liked - pickles, black olives, and barbeque potato chips. Everything Lennon wanted was strong in flavor because the medication killed his taste buds.

He loved cream of mushroom soup. We put together a cream of mushroom soup, mashed potatoes and mustard concoction. He ate it all by himself, thankfully. I didn't have to try a bite.

Watching my son eats this way was weird. I was cooking healthy food for me, Little Kevin, Jarod and Big Kevin -- Very little canned or boxed food. But Lennon couldn't get energy from protein like we could, so he ate candy and processed food - anything to get the calories.

Lennon had to drink a prescription formula every day to give him amino acids and take 18 pills a day. Of course, Lennon would spit out the formula. So sometimes we made our own "formula ice cream," frozen with chocolate syrup and water. It worked, sometimes. Lennon's pills we had to crush because they were too big for a 4 year old to swallow them. He absolutely hated the medication but, on most days, was a trooper and took them the first time. Other days, however, I tried the trick we all use when giving medicine to a dog or cat - burying the pill in something tasty like cheese.

In Germany we used Liverwurst. For Lennon, it was applesauce, chocolate pudding and even grape jelly. Three times a day.

In December 2007, I enrolled into a master's program to study Mental Health Counseling. Life is simply too short and we should continually follow our dreams. I chose counseling because of my roots as a foster child. Growth happens if you are open to it and when the tools are provided. I knew what it was like to not talk about my problems and when I was younger, I wish I had. I wanted to help other foster children.

After four months of stability, Lennon had another huge ammonia spike in January 2008 that was in the 200's, more than 325% higher than a normal level.

No one was really clear about why, except that it flushed out some of the edemas on his brain. It was almost like a bubble burst and gushed the ammonia in his system, so his body was reacting to the normal symptoms of being ill. Thankfully, the episode was the beginning of Lennon's vision gradually improving.

The next six months, we lived our routine of going to school, regulating diet and managing medication. The kids would be playing board games in their rooms, or go outside in the afternoons just hanging out on the trampoline. My partner would help take care of cleaning, laundry and preparing food for the family and Lennon. On several occasions, the whole family hiked the scenic Skyline Drive, with a few abrupt early departures for Lennon's symptoms.

All of a sudden, in August 2008, we were back to the hospital twice a month. Lennon's ammonia levels were just over the safe limit, in the 100s. But the reality is it doesn't matter how elevated the ammonia is because the brain takes a hit every single time.

Lennon was already significantly cognitively delayed and required occupational therapy, physical therapy, speech therapy and vision assistance. Even though his vision slowly returned, he still required extensive support to get around.

We stayed in the hospital for a few days each time; usually I had to handle these visits on my own because Big Kevin was at home with the other kids. On a few of those visits, Lennon and I spent 15 hours to 24 hours in the emergency room. I would in the room up with one angry child, who at 4 years old required a crib to be safe. Instead, I had to wrestle him constantly because, once you are in the emergency room, they only check on you periodically to give you an update on when a hospital room is available.

Finally, admitted long enough for the ammonia to be 88, just a few units high, and then cleared to go home. Lennon was incredibly scared, fighting the nurses and me. I can only imagine how scary it must be for a toddler who cannot fully grasp what is going on.

Over time, the doctors and I made the decision to give Lennon an IV port, a device placed under the skin into a vein to speed access for blood work and medicine. This helped shorten the days in the hospital. Occasionally we weren't even admitted if the ammonia levels could come down in the emergency room using the port.

Urea Cycle Disorder became harder and harder to manage. The more time we spent in the hospital, the less I saw Little Kevin, Big Kevin and Jarod. How was I to split myself up between the three boys? In the end it came down to keeping Lennon alive. I hoped that my boys would understand this and not hold it against me. I wavered through each day, questioning my skills as a parent. Finally, I started a blog to help me process and not hold in what happened on any given day. It was a good way update friends and family who did not exactly live close by. Most of my family is in Germany and his dad side of the family lived 3-5 hours away.

And, the blog was, is a therapeutic way to release and share my and Lennon's experiences. . For the most part I wanted to keep the blog very matter of fact because I found it incredibly difficult to show how hard this really was for me.

Some days, Lennon was doing increasingly well. It would appear that our home routine was working. A good day meant that Lennon was gentle and kind and he loved. He would swing his arms around and tell me "love u". He would love the cats and the dogs, use them as pillows instead of punching bags. During those good days, Lennon was able to go to school, in hopes that he could and would learn. It was far too soon to tell the lasting damage the high ammonia episodes had done to his precious brain.

Yet, when you live in constant crisis, you just could not relax for a minute.

I wondered when and what would cause his ammonia levels to go up again. Was there a better way to manage it all just a little better at home? I felt that if we could get his diet under control more, we could stabilize the early symptoms sooner, but we could never be sure of this. My reality was that I could not leave Lennon out of sight for a single moment, because each moment became about keeping him alive.

It was sometimes difficult to fathom that Lennon was five years old. His social delays were so apparent that independent play was not something he knew how to do. I assumed he liked school and was grateful that, for the moment, he didn't realize his own delays and how much harder he had to work on his academics. Lennon was to repeat pre-kindergarten just to give him some extra time. Lennon's learning took him about 6 months longer than the average child when asked how old he was, Lennon would continue to respond, he was four, even though he had turned five just a few months prior. The odd thing was that he could remember going to the zoo. When you would ask him what elephants do, he would tell you "they poop".

There were moments I wondered if I was holding him back too much and not giving him enough credit. He was able to feed himself and walk without too many struggles.

I tried to stay busy because, given too much time, I would over think and worry. Worry about other children bullying him. Worry about him not ever catching up and always delayed. My heart ached and my mind wondered, why my son? I felt anger and frustration, questioning what had I done to have an ill child?

But those moments don't last for long. You have to get up and keep on getting it. I didn't have time to wallow in self-pity. I had a kid to keep alive and boys to love and show them that life isn't miserable despite the challenges. None of us in the family ever had time to relax. Any minute, Lennon's fearlessness combined with a lack of impulse control and aggression would find us chasing him as he ran out into the street or climbed on top of the refrigerator at 2 o'clock in the morning. Lennon could not understand consequences. Parenting healthy children was challenging enough and it was just so much more complicated with Lennon.

Lennon changed his mind every minute (and this is the truth). Diagnosed with Attention-Deficit Hyperactivity Disorder (ADHD). ADHD causes you to not be able to focus, overactive, unable to control behavior, or a combination of these. The Doctor prescribed Adderall to manage the symptoms, which posed another challenge. Most ADHD medications suppress appetite. For a kid with a rare genetic disorder who needs calories, this was going one more bump in the road.

His behavior was so uncontrollable even at lower levels of the ammonia. It was frustrating that I couldn't help him. I can't change his behavior instantly, and it seemed

Lennon's brain didn't allow him to change either. Lennon's hospital visits became more frequent. His behavior was so uncontrollable even at lower levels of the ammonia and it is frustrating. It was frustrating because you couldn't help him, you can't change it instantly and his brain doesn't allow him to change it. It can be very nerve wracking and wearing on one's patience when your child changes his or her mind every minute (and this is the truth).

As a mother, faced with constant decisions. With Lennon's increasingly frequent hyper ammonia episodes, doctors suggested a port to speed up Lennon's treatments, a feeding tube (G-tube). But a kid like Lennon could pull it out, which could cause infections. I wanted to think that he'd surprise me and perhaps leave the G-Tube alone, but I had little faith in that.

In and out of the hospital – trapped in a cycle, we would never get out of. Financially things were brutal. I had to feed the six of us for under $10.00 a day. Even with both Big Kevin and me working, there just didn't seem enough money. Then a local church gave us a deep freezer and loaded it up with food.

Other fears crept up. Little Kevin struggled in school. Jarod struggled more and more with my attention focusing on Lennon. The school system assigned Jarod and Little Kevin an educational support specialist to help them at least through the school. My partner's daughter, Katie, was unwavering through it all, continued with her grades. I loved that she started to connect with art and I felt a small piece of pride that I may be in some tiny place had something to do with that by crocheting and wood-burning and always sharing and encouraging creative.

Some days it took all that I had to care for my family and still complete my homework for my Masters Degree in Counseling. I have always loved psychology so wrote my papers with ease. It was, along with my crochet and wood burning, my time away from reality.

Yet no matter how hard I tried to distract myself, the urea cycle disorder controlled our life.

One second Lennon was fine and the next, I found myself driving 40 minutes into town to the hospital.

Once, admitted to the hospital with an ammonia level of 237. The doctors and nurses followed standard procedure and administered the lipid and dextrose treatment. Initially it appeared to work, as his ammonia was going down to 147. We assumed we would go home the following day.

Not so fast! After the next blood draw his ammonia came back 353! Levels that high damage the brain every single time, sending my kid into a medical crisis. Lennon was transferred to the PICU so that he could receive more concentrated medication through his port.

This damn disorder is so scary because you realize that that you really could be losing your child. I knew he might not make it despite the medical care and everything else we were doing to keep him alive.

Despite his behavioral issues due to the brain damage and his delayed development, he was such a gentle soul. He loved and was fun and kept my life interesting. He adored his older siblings and wanted their attention all the time.

Too often during this time my self-care was falling by the wayside. It took constant reminders that in order to take care of my son; I had to take care of myself. I longed normal days of family time, struggle to pay our bills and to put food on the table, as opposed to being on the 7th floor in the hospital.

I thrived on connection with other Urea Cycle Disorder families through blogging. As I was sharing the challenges we were enduring, members of the community reached out and shared with me, like Jim.

"Just wanted to let you know I just read this entire blog and my thoughts and prayers are with Lennon right now, and with you and the rest of your family. Life certainly is not always easy. Our son has UCD, and though we have

never come close to losing him, we have had to deal with his affliction, him, and our emotions regarding the situation. So, while I cannot know the full degree of your pain, I can feel it." (Jim 9/16/2008)

Trying to explain Urea Cycle Disorder to someone from the outside is damn hard. When I received blog comments, I knew that I wasn't alone. There is something to be said about people walking the same or similar path who can connect to you that can be comforting. Connecting with others who get it first hand was much more profound than I could have imagined.

I needed that support. There didn't appear a way to control Lennon's ammonia any longer. Lennon and I were at the hospital 2 or 3 times a week in order to check his levels. Every reading was well over the 200's - usually in the 300's - and the results were heartbreaking.

Lennon was not mentally coherent, unable to recognize where he was. Once he had to be sedated because he was so agitated the doctors feared he would pull his IV out. Dr. W, the geneticist, became increasingly concerned that Lennon's Urea cycle disorder was becoming medically unmanageable and that he could end up in a coma or worse. He suggested a liver transplant. While it is no cure, a new organ would save Lennon's life.

But a transplant would weaken Lennon's immune

system. There is a higher risk for infections and other illnesses, as well as possible rejection of the liver. So we would replace one medical situation with a different one. It was difficult to really wrap my head around all of this information. At the same time, I could look back on what Lennon had already survived. A transplant was not out the question.

There comes a point in parenting where you look at your kids and you find their strength. For Lennon it was being able to watch him and this disorder while for Jarod it was trying to fit in with his friends despite his red hair, and for Kevin it was just trying to find his place in this world. The boys, thankfully, got that I needed to be with Lennon because it was a matter of life and death. I secretly longed for the day I could just be a mom who loved her children and was able to show that I would have done the same exact thing for Jarod or Little Kevin, had it been one of them.

Big Kevin and I rotated shifts so that one of us was always at the hospital while the other one worked and checked on the other kids at home. And as tough as the travel and cost and fear and uncertainty were on our family, we did what we had to. There was no time to wallow in pity. I cherished every moment that all of my kids were healthy and every time we laughed and had fun together.

When I went into work, people asked why I was not in the hospital with Lennon. As if my bills would pay themselves. It was a relief being at work. It was a distraction from keeping Lennon calm, which really was a job in itself. I was tired more days that I care to think about. I would go days without seeing my home, sleeping in my bed or even hugging my children.

Someone mentioned to me I should receive a "Super Mom" award, between caring for Lennon, going to school, working, maintaining a relationship and still somehow manage raising my other kids. To stay a functioning human being, I had to be busy and do things. On the days I had the time, I crocheted or created wood burnings. I had to channel my energy into various projects, because if I didn't, I would simply fall apart. September 22, 2008 we sent notification to the transplant team that we want Lennon to be evaluated for a liver transplant. Now we waited for them to determine if it is even worth an evaluation.

Was this the right decision?

Would this really save his life?

I was heading to bed when I heard some commotion and, sure enough, there was Lennon holding his blanket, rambling things that didn't make sense. He had vomited. I drove him into town in the rain. I hate driving at night, I don't like driving in the rain and I don't like driving at night in the rain.

We did the normal routine -- emergency room, blood draw, get cozy in a room, and wait. Ammonia level five times too high – 309! It took all I had to breathe!
It was now too common to see Lennon drool when he was sick, a sign that his brain was shutting down.
The liver transplant began to make more and more sense to me.

On September 28th, 2008, I wrote the following blog entry:
"I feel like the world, no not the world but Lennon, is slipping away from me underneath my hands. It seems no matter what we do at home and the best care everyone gives to him, it doesn't matter. I want to hang on to hope and find the strength that he will survive and that he will be there, graduate from elementary School, middle school and high school. But also that he is enjoying life, finding the right partner for him...all the things we wish that our children should accomplish to achieve their happiness. I am barely hanging on to that hope."

My partner and I couldn't find the time to breathe, let alone spend time together. The kids were hurting not only because my partner and I were not home consistently (though he saw them more than me) and they too were worried about their little brother. Prayer chains were all over the world to keep the faith and to keep the hope that Lennon will come out of this crazy thing called urea cycle disorder.

This disorder was so damn hard. Lennon alternated between mentally incoherent and "hitting, kicking, biting and attempting to run away. The doctors had to sedate him more frequently just so that he could receive the medication to counteract the genetic disorder
I attempted to explain to Lennon was going on with him and what was about to happen, but Lennon didn't understand a thing. Sure he heard the words, but didn't comprehend the meaning. I wanted to hug him to help him be calm when he required medical attention. I still have a scar from a previous hyper-ammonia episode where Lennon bit me in my shoulder due to his aggression, a side effect of the urea cycle disorder. When the ammonia is elevated, it messed with Lennon's brain every single time, and each time his brain suffered more damage.

Then, even at levels in his safe zone, he became increasingly violent, uncooperative, and not listening. It felt like two personalities possessed Lennon: one moment he was sweet and loving Lennon, and the next he was the holy terror where trying to bite you and fight you in every way he could.

I felt like he was slipping away from me, despite his

fighting spirit. He will not go down easy! The Angel of Death will just have to wait a bit longer.

When Lennon was well, he loved to sit in my lap and be cuddled. He didn't care if I was crocheting or not, he wanted my attention and he got it. He sat in a laundry basket and ate his grapes because he decided it was a good place to be in that moment in time. He wore funny orange troll wigs on his head because it was just the thing to do.

Due to frequent changes in Lennon's behavior, the geneticist and medical team thought it would be a good idea to have him admitted to the Kluge Children's Rehabilitation Center (KCRC) for a Neuro-Developmental observation. Unfortunately, Medicaid did not approve the request. This was tough, because it was difficult to figure out what behavior was ammonia related and what part was just typical for his age. I received a phone call from the school because my 5 year old was hitting the other children and pulling their hair. I cried. He loves people and he loved his peers.

I found myself increasingly overwhelmed. There was so much pressure in keeping Lennon healthy and meeting the demands of life. Managing to study for my master's program and taking care of the kids and keeping my partner happy was a juggling act. I had no time to breathe. I had no idea how to stop worrying or letting go of the anxiety.

For a week we had managed to stay out of the emergency room and Lennon looked really good. His personality was back - the sassy, funny little guy who keeps you on your toes. I watched him play with a white piece of PVC pipe. He slipped it on his arm and with the biggest smile on his face he struck a warrior pose and said "charge". He had the biggest laugh as if it was the funniest thing he had ever experienced.

Being home was welcome relief. I checked Lennon's pupils at the end of my workday – because if his ammonia levels were elevated, his pupils would get big. His pupils looked normal.

Things only stayed well for a short time before we found ourselves back in the emergency room with another hyper-ammonia episode. While we were hanging out around UVA, the initial meeting with the transplant team happened just like a regular routine visit. The doctors explained what the process is to get on the transplant list, and what life is after transplant.

I was scared and worried about the risk related to the transplant. The decision was to give Lennon a whole or partial liver from a cadaver. Due to the genetic connection of the urea cycle disorder, a living donation was out of the questions, especially since there is a risk that it won't "cure" the urea cycle disorder.

The doctors reviewed Lennon's medical history, gave x-rays, and took an ultrasound of his liver. Then the doctors had their meeting of the minds.

They asked me a gazillion more questions about his development and home life. The process felt so matter of fact but my insides were churning. I felt exposed and bare.

And then the doctors left. They had to decide whether or not to approve Lennon being listed for a liver. The transplant team uses a scoring system to predict how healthy the patient will be in 3 months. Once on the list, the patient is re-evaluated every 30 days with blood work, and his or her current condition is weighed along with how long the patient has been on the list.

The doctor called me at home to let us now that Lennon had been listed for a new liver and that he will be on the transplant list in about 3-4 weeks. It was just a few days later that we received an official letter making this more official and real.

I tried to imagine how life would be different without the urea cycle disorder.

I tried imagining life with a new liver and all the food options that would become available to Lennon.

It is really hard to not think about what could happen if things don't go well. What if he doesn't make it through the surgery? What if the liver will not work?
We immediately began to live life on standby. We could receive a phone call at any time, on any day.

And then I realized we haven't stayed overnight in the hospital even once for the last three weeks. Unreal. Lennon had hard time being satisfied. "Hungry mommy" came across his lips and we played the "guess what Lennon wants to eat" game for about 5 minutes or so. Once we won the prize of knowing, we fixed his food and then he didn't want it.

This was the real frustrating part on our daily routines. You monitor his food, make suggestions of what he can have, he decides on something but then does not eat it. Then you have to make sure he does eat and drink, because when he stops, his ammonia will go up.
While Lennon was well, he attended school. It was the time of the year where his teacher and the school were trying to create a plan for the following school year. He was nowhere near ready to go to kindergarten, but he could not be held back. No medication (as of yet) had worked to keep him focused on anything more than 5 minutes and his progress in learning had been incredibly slow.

Lennon was delayed in his maturity although he was

about 2 years behind his peers. His speech, while not perfect, had improved tremendously. He was talking in small 3-4 word sentences.

Lennon also became easily obsessed with one thing and found it difficult that it wouldn't happen when he expected it, especially playing video games. When he did get to play his game, he couldn't stick with just one game. One minute he wants to play Sponge-bob and the next minute he changed it to the spider-man game.
I wondered if Lennon knew how much the genetic disorder impacted his life and if he had an idea that each moment could be his last. I wondered if Lennon knew that he was different or that he couldn't do the things his peers did.

The hospital had become such an integrated part of our life that Lennon found it difficult to accept that he was not being admitted.

Part Three

October 29th, 2008 it was official. Lennon was on top the transplant list.

Breathe!

Now we had to be patient, keeping Lennon healthy and be grateful. Which is worse, waiting for the liver or fear the surgery itself?

My gratitude went out to the donor that would be saving my son's life. Medical technology is amazing, but there is nothing more amazing than a person being an organ donor so that another person may live. I am an organ donor; please do consider being one too.
I know sometimes religion; personal beliefs and life get in the way - but what an amazing gift to give - LIFE. As I sat down, writing my thoughts to the world on the blog, I knew that giving birth is giving life and it is quite miraculous. The liver donor would give the gift of continuing life.

I pondered what life might be after the surgery. We hoped that the UCD would be cured, and that Lennon would lead a normal and healthy life. The questions swirled: will he recover from some of the brain damage he has suffered? Would he catch up in his development? Would some of the behaviors go away -- high anxiety, the obsessions?

Lennon's neuro-developmental and behavioral doctor recommended an antipsychotic medication that is sometimes used for children with obsessive compulsive and other behavioral challenges. It works by changing the actions of chemicals in the brain to help with some of his behavioral issues we were coping with. It worked beautifully! We thought at first... unfortunately, it actually worked too well because it covered up all the symptoms that would let us know that his ammonia was elevated.

Lennon had not been sleeping well but usually settled in, once I was home from work. He went to school like on most good days but had to be picked up within two hours. Lennon had the shakes and I made call to Neuro-Development.

Instinct told me we should also check his ammonia and we went in for blood work, waiting for about two hours. Lennon's ammonia level was 269! And instead of his levels coming down after his treatment regimen, his levels climbed up to 290.

This medication that appeared to be a miracle in its own way, covered his typical symptoms of lack of intake, lethargy, aggression, mental alertness. I did notice that he drooled some, which in the recent month had been an indication that his brain is shutting down. Lennon also had shakes that made me nervous, which were a side effect from the medication.

I decided to keep Lennon of any kind of behavioral and ADHD medication for the time being, preparing myself for a more impulsive running out the door, climbing on the couch, playing superman.

I kept thinking and wondering about how long has his ammonia been high and we didn't know this time.
While Lennon was being treated for his high ammonia, I talked to the transplant coordinator! She mentioned that on it's been 30 days since being listed and that his score would increase, this meant that "the call" would happen soon after.
You know the wish that Lennon can be relatively healthy and live a relatively normal life.

I say relative because the reality is he has suffered brain damage and he is behind in social age appropriate development. He has a difficult time maintaining personal space, he finds it difficult to maintain within boundaries and rules that are given. Making friends is very difficult for him as he plays next to your rather than with you.

Unfortunately, you cannot indicate the permanency of this brain damage. MRI's and CAT Scans can indicate some of the damaged areas, but in some areas the brain can heal itself and it is so hard to predict what his brain will recover from. One thing is clear, the ADHD and some of his anxiety and obsessive-compulsive issues are permanent.

We made it home on a Saturday and settled into our normal. Goofing around playing baseball in the yard. Playing outside as a family together was a rarity with my work hours being 3 p.m. to 11 p.m. and I miss a lot of the afternoon fun.

Lennon appeared to be crankier than usual and aggressive. His outbursts are unreasonable but then he is 5 and at 5 everything tends to be unreasonable (keeping in mind his delays his behavior is quite typical for the terrible threes).

He wants what he wants, when he wants it, NOW. He wants to play video games, he wants candy, he wants mommy to hold him, he wants to color, he wants to go outside, he wants chips, he wants dinner, he wants to watch cartoons, he wants to play with cars, he wants to go to school. He wants to do all of these things in 10 minutes or less.

One Saturday he wanted to go to school and it was hard for him to understand that there is no school on the weekend.

Lennon: no school because I have a headache?

Me: Uhh no, you don't have school because it's the weekend. There is not school this weekend.

Lennon: You need to call the doctors because I have a headache

Me: But I think you are fine and we don't need to call the doctor

Lennon: no my head hurts; I need an IV in my IV Port
He complains about his head or his eye and I do believe that he hurts, but I can't convince him that we don't always need to go to the doctors.

***

I maintained a blog for our journey along the way, to vent and to update family and friends that couldn't be with us. The posts went from almost daily to every few weeks, pending Lennon's medical situation. What you are reading now are excerpts from the blog.

***

November 18th, 2008 I lay in bed when my phone rang at an ungodly hour.

We have a match, please stay close to home as we will call you back to let you know when you should come into the hospital.

Jumping out of bed with a million thoughts in my head. There were phone calls to make. Ensuring his bag was ready to go.

Don't forget the cat - never forget his cat, the stuffed animal he has had since he was three months old that was bought during a shopping spree at Halloween time. Did I mention Halloween is his favorite day of the year?
I called his dad, work and the school of course.

I attempted to do schoolwork but my phone rang again: "please come in now we are ready to make this happen"! My heart raced a million miles a minute as we were heading to the hospital. Here it goes, the moment our life will change again forever.

Arriving at the hospital, we immediately went into the pre-operation where the doctors and nurses were getting him ready for the surgery. The doctors recapping the plan of action, and a few signatures here and there for consent to move forward, Lennon was on his way to the OR.
I had a hard time keeping it together, as he was wheeled into the operating room. I told myself to be strong. I couldn't show how scared I was, wondering if he would make it out of the surgery. I placed my faith into the universe and sat with his dad in the waiting room.
In the waiting room, another family was waiting for their child to come out of a difficult surgery. They offered prayers for Lennon and my faith in humanity was healed just a little more. A touching moment and so heartfelt, I couldn't believe strangers could be so giving during their

own challenging times.

Three hours later, Lennon was in his room in the PICU, when chaos broke lose and he was headed back into the OR for emergency surgery, a problem with the connectivity of the artery.

Wednesday, November 19, 2008

Lennon's artery was not functioning as well as it should. He was on a blood thinner to help remove a clot however, after another ultrasound this morning; only half of the connections were working. The emergency surgery did not work and he is at risk for abscess, infection and organs dying off. Lennon was relisted for another liver. And so we wait again!

During our waiting period, the doctors brought Lennon out of his medically induced coma. "I'm thirsty" was Lennon's first response once the breathing tube was removed. He didn't understand why he needed to wait for a drink.

He looks really good though. His eyes aren't dilated from stressing; his skin is pink and warm to the touch. He isn't all that pretty, I mean handsome due to puffiness a lovely side effect from sedation.

It is so frustrating to wait! I cannot express my gratitude

for the first donor family and unfortunately the next one to come. I cannot describe how this feels.

The reality is a baby has died, but has given life to my son, even for just a short time. It is unreal. It is an unselfish act and I thank them from the bottom of my heart. The outreach to my family also has been amazing. We have prayer chains all over the world. WOW!

Thank you! Thank you for having the faith and trust that he will be okay. Thank you for the emotional support!

Friday, November 21, 2008

The phone call came, we have another liver and surgery is scheduled for 11 a.m.

Lennon went into surgery at 1:00 p.m. today. He was not feeling well and was in a lot of pain from the first surgery. He looks exhausted. Let's hope and pray and give positive thoughts that this surgery will go great, that everything will be functioning like it is supposed to and that he can soon be as healthy as he should be.

Monday, November 24, 2008 ~ Things are looking up
The transplant surgery on Friday went well. However, due to the extensive trauma and swelling from the surgery, the incision area left open over the weekend. He was sedated and on the breathing machine. His liver enzymes are coming down which is a good thing and means that his liver is slowly but surely adjusting and working in him.

There is a concern about his kidney as his urination decreased. On some levels this is okay as his body is adjusting but some of his other lab numbers are completely out of whack.

This morning they took him back to the OR and closed his abdomen. Funny thing, just before they were worried about his urine about it, apparently Lennon found relief during the surgery.

Lennon will come out of sedation at around 1:00 p.m. and be taken off the breathing tube.

Lennon is a pretty lucky guy. He continues to defy them every step of the way. I am honored to be his mom. I believe that he will do something great and important with his life.

I am just amazed that he has received not one but two livers in one week.

Thanks to everyone that has send us his or her prayers and thoughts; that has helped me and my family financially, emotionally and in every other step of the way.

Wednesday, November 26, 2008

On Monday when they took out the breathing tube, it appeared that Lennon was not ready. I consider myself a strong person, but I was not prepared to watch my son not breathe. My heart hurt, and I never knew this kind of pain before. Lennon's dad and I were ushered to the lounge and asked to wait. Excruciating! It was like an eternity before they allowed us back to his room, with Lennon breathing.

Sobbing I thanked the universe.

During the night Lennon struggling to breathe and the oxygen indicator showing he did not receive enough CO_2. His numbers fluctuated from 67-91, normal is 100. The CO_2 sensor measures the oxygen in our blood. I heard him say "save me mommy, save me." I paged the nurse and stood by his bed. Holding him, I silently cried wishing I could help him.

One of his lungs had partially collapsed and there was fluid interfering with breathing. Lennon was not ready to breathe on his own.

I must trust that he will do things on his terms, when he's ready. This is Lennon!

Yesterday I went home and hung out with my other kids, did some homework and cuddled with the dogs. I took a much-needed shower and sat at my desk to study for a while before sinking into my chair to crochet. The older kids watched television. I think the important part was I was there for them and available if they needed me. I also need to rest. Close to exhaustion, because I wouldn't be any good to Lennon.

The support from our community has been overwhelming. We appreciate everything and anything that comes our way. One of my partner's friends had brought us thanksgiving dinner to the hospital and a local church was providing our family with food. The thought to make things easier for us is so unreal. We realize that now is where we need the help, even though we have a hard time asking.

Sunday, November 30, 2008

Lennon is doing better. His liver function is working towards normal. His kidneys look good and his lungs are better. They are weaning him of the breathing machine so that he breathes on his own.

He has a long recovery ahead but everyone (from the professional perspective) is positive and confident that things are definitely and finally heading into the right direction. Some of you who follow this blog, sorry for not calling etc. but I know everyone understands the money is tight and times are stressful. I do appreciate everyone's positive thoughts and energy in my son's recovery.

Monday, December 01, 2008

Lennon needed more draining tubes, as he accumulated too much fluid around the abdomen and pulmonary section. His white blood cell count went up and he is on antibiotics to help fight possible infections. In addition he is on diuretics to remove excess fluid that has developed in his body.

His ammonia is 60 today.

Other levels are also coming down indicating that the liver is slowly starting to do its job.
YAY!

He is awake, and though can't talk quite yet handles everything pretty darn well. What a trooper dealing with the restraints, the oxygen going up his nose, draining tubes on the side of his body and several IV's. He is certainly a hero to many people and I am amazing how strong his will to live is.

There is no game plan on how soon he will go home, but there is hope that it will be before Christmas. Our tree was not going up until he goes home.

The tough part is that I am going back to work tomorrow. I love the place of employment and my colleagues!

From the supervisors willing to work with me while some have donated their PTO time so not only could I say with Lennon but also I still get a paycheck! Thanks to anyone that has donated some of their hours to me so that I may care for Lennon in his recovery. You people are the best!

Be thankful for all you have in your life, take nothing for granted. Know that people care, and it doesn't matter how close or far you are from them physically or any other way.

Wednesday, December 03, 2008

We are moving towards recovery. They want Lennon to eat, drink and be jolly?

Well, not so fact. His throat hurts from removing the breathing tube. He is not talking nor eating. It's time to get creative, perhaps some oatmeal or a milkshake. Wow, a milkshake! Something he couldn't have before because of the urea cycle disorder. Now that he had the new liver however, he was free to eat what ever he liked. Does he even care for them is the question. We will be exploring his new food options the minute he's up for that. On the way positive side, his liver is functioning!!!

Saturday, December 06, 2008

Nothing ever goes as smooth as you hope. A repeat ultrasound found that the portal vein is clotted. The portal vein is essential as it transports oxygen-depleted blood from the stomach, intestines, spleen, gallbladder and the pancreas to the liver. They can't do surgery on it, and said that this can happen from time to time. This could cause problems later on down the road, and mean he may need another liver transplant. The team recommended that he takes heparin, a blood thinner for 6 months in hopes that the clot will go away.

Overall everyone is pleased with his progress and are making a big deal about how good he looks. My personal thing is that he is warm. Something unreal because due toe the urea cycle disorder, his body was always cold to the touch.

Tuesday, December 09, 2008

Right now, food is going to be a challenge. His body just underwent a huge adjustment. It's a new him. If we think about what the ammonia has done before, I wonder if he feels weird now.

Normal the new weird!

In the past, Lennon has not liked foods intuitively,

usually those high in protein. I always wondered why he didn't like chicken nuggets or fish sticks. There were even some vegetables he didn't eat: corn, peas and carrots. He loves starches but not spaghetti.

Lennon is drinking water but the doctors want him to have drinks with more nutritional values. Meeting Lennon's nutritional needs and allowing Lennon to move at its own pace, now there's a challenge.

On a positive note, two draining tubes were removed and he was moved out of the PICU. He will need two shots of heparin and his regular meds for the transplant (steroids, anti rejection). By next week this time we truly could be home. Well, all they have to do is get his dosage correct and remove one more draining tube.
Are we going to be home for Christmas?

Sunday, December 14, 2008

Lennon was in his room for two hours before he was back in the PICU. His potassium was super high and he was at risk for seizures. They observed him for a few hours and noted that they needed to stabilize his electrolytes.

On Wednesday, Lennon took a dive and became mentally incoherent. A CT Scan was done to ensure that he was not bleeding on his brain due to being on a blood thinner.

The brain Is fine, but his CO2 is out of whack. Lennon quit eating, drinking, everything was no, he didn't want to walk; he didn't want to do anything. His mental state did not improve; he's been calling my name non-stop for about 3 das now. In hopes that it would help they removed a draining tube but immediately his oxygen dropped. An X-ray showed that Lennon has fluid on the lungs that impacted his breathing. A new draining tube was placed to continue to drain off the fluid accumulated in his body and success was noted! All of this fluid issue did not help him wanting to eat or drink.

If Lennon does not start eating, he will need to be fed with a NG tube through his nose. He needs to food so that his body can heal, food that contains protein. The concept of Lennon eating protein makes me nervous since it was the underlying reason for him being ill with vomiting, lethargy and psychosis for five years.

His ammonia has been in the 50's – 90's. Unreal. It was frustrating when no one cold tell us anything about was going on with Lennon. No one would come talk to us about why he was acting so odd and what the doctors would do about it. Lennon was in a different world, absent minded if you will. Lennon continued to be full of fluid and not urinate enough.

One of the challenges is we have two different teams that

don't agree on a treatment plan. In the PICU he's stuck in bed without the ability to really get around. He's hooked up to wires so that the monitor can watch his heart rate, oxygen level and blood pressure.

I believe that if Lennon had the opportunity to be on the floor, he would take steps to improve.

With all the hospital visits in the past, I believe that his mood is impacted having to be stuck in bed. Part of me was relieved for the close observation while another wished for the freedom on the regular hospital floor. My sunny little boy was missing. He was sad, so very very sad.
I wish there is more communication, a smidgen of an idea about his mental state or lack of interest in food. I wish that the PICU and the Transplant team could just collaborate and agree on something. The Transplant team has the ultimate say in Lennon's care, but the PICU is observing him a 100% of the time. I don't mean to make this a negative venting session, but how can Lennon progress if no one agrees on how to medically support him.

Friday, December 19, 2008

Infections creep up.

Lennon had an MRI on Tuesday for his brain and his abdomen.

His brain is fine, his abdomen not so much. They found a 6 cm fluid pocket behind the liver.

He was back on the breathing tube and a draining tube for the fluid pocket. The doctors are not positive that the breathing tube will come out because he has about 2 liters of excess fluid.

The fluid behind his liver is infected - because the liver oozed due to being a partial liver. The oozing caused particles to be left behind that have become infected. At some point during our stay at hotel hospital, Lennon contracted C.Diff. My understanding is that our guts have good and bad bacteria, and C.Diff happens when the bad bacteria wins. Until the C.Diff is cleared, Lennon will be under contact precautions as it is contagious. In addition, the fluid that is slowly draining from his body also is infected and he will receive more specialized antibiotics. Hoping the breathing tube will come out soon and that he can start feeling better. His electrolytes have finally mellowed out and his blood levels and number are also improving.

Here's to Lennon feeling better and being himself more and more each day!

Monday, December 22, 2008

The fluid pocket that behind his liver definitely has a virus. It is called VRE (vancomycin-resistant enterococci) and is resistant to most treatment. People who have had surgery, have no immune system are at risk to contract VRE. So they are giving him antibiotics but it can take quite some time weeks to months before this virus is out of his system.

VRE is passed on from health professionals when a specific antibiotic like vancomycin (hence the name) is used. Lennon has been on this specific medication for a few weeks now.

While he's contact precaution i.e. the nurses and doctors will have to wear additional yellow gown and gloves before entering the room. Washing hands is critical for everyone o that it is not passed on to others. He is still on the breathing tube but that may come out today or tomorrow. If I had a guess tomorrow seems more likely.

Thursday, December 25, 2008

Thoughts and prayers have been heard.
Lennon is off the breathing tube, but still struggles to breathe, as he is still so full of fluid on the inside. He has a mask on his little face that is too big, to give him oxygen. All of his numbers (liver, kidney and blood) look

good, probably the best they have been. His ammonia has been 31, which is the lowest that it probably has ever been in his lifetime.

His body and mind are taking their time to heal and recover. Every now and again his eyes will open ever so slightly before he drifts off back to sleep. His hand will move in hopes to find another hand or his beloved stuffed cat.

I was asked if I regret the decision to have the transplant. Nope! The alternative looks far worse.

Not having the transplant could have meant brain damage, coma or even death. I like life more. My objective is to continue to trust the doctors on this journey. Keep the faith and hang onto the belief that he will be okay. He will walk out of here one day. He is destined to be on this earth for the greater good. Without the trusting into the universe I would not be able to hang one and my demise would be his demise.

Sunday, December 28, 2008

Lennon has been on C-Pap, a machine that helps keep the airways open. They did another CT scan and his right lung is completely whited out and causing him to have difficulties breathing.

His CO2 is high enough that they think he may need to go back on the breathing machine.

The doctors are also considering a procedure in which a small video camera and a suction instrument will go in and clear the fluid pockets. Everyone agrees that if we can get the fluid under control, he will start to feel better because his kidneys and liver are functioning.

Tuesday, December 30, 2008

We received an official diagnosis today from his liver biopsy. The specific Urea Cycle Disorder is called Carbamoyl Phosphate Synthetase Deficiency I (CPS I). CPS deficiency is when an enzyme is missing that indicates the path for incorporation of ammonia. CPS deficiency is rare, 1 in 56000 and mortality and morbidity rates are high. Untreated CPS deficiency is likely fatal. Symptoms related to CPS I: Anorexia, Irritability, Heavy or rapid breathing, Lethargy, Vomiting, Disorientation, Somnolence, Asterixis (rare), Combativeness, Obtundation, Coma, Cerebral edema, death

Now I know more than ever that I have made the right decision to transplant. Lennon's geneticist speculated that he had CPS 1.

Tuesday, December 30, 2008

Only he has the power to convince the docs he doesn't need much, just time.

The other day the doctors talked about the video-scope but decided that in the mean time they add medication to the chest tube to help break up any clots that may hinder drainage. Voila we have fluid movement and his X-Ray has much improved.

Lennon has the will and the power to fight. He is off the C-PAP and on the small nose oxygen and his numbers keep looking better.
With all the narcotics Lennon had on board due keep him sedated, he is now experiencing withdrawal symptoms. The poor kid is vomiting and shaking. It is hard to get on top of withdrawal effects if you don't catch them in time. He is slowly becoming more mobile, allowing fluid to move around. At the moment, he is resting.

Saturday, January 03, 2009

Lennon is on the high flow oxygen with the cannula tubing. The cannula goes around his face, tucks in behind his ear, with two small tube ends in his nose. He is receiving most of his nutrition from NG tube. Unfortunately he's been vomiting on and off because there is fluid causing pressure on his stomach. It's a mystery why his body isn't absorbing the fluid. Lennon is cranky and the methadone helps him to maintain mellowness. Come to think of it, the vomiting could also be due to the withdrawals that he's going through. I asked the doctor why he was vomiting and his response: that is a good question.

Perhaps she wasn't the right doctor to ask. Lennon has a lot of people in his car.

Monday, January 05, 2009

Lennon is more awake the days and attempts to speak. "Mommy lay in the bed with me" or "I'm thirsty". This is a YAY moment for sure.

One of the issues is that Lennon has ascites, which is an abnormal fluid collection in his abdomen. To add to the challenge is that Lennon isn't urinating enough and to help him they give him albumin, a protein in plasma. It helps to keep the fluid in the vessels rather than out. Lennon had a CT scan with contrast to figure out where all this fluid was leaking from within his body. One part to the problem that is also a solution is movement. He's not moving enough.

All I want is for my kid to feel better, so we can go home. Living in the hospital is no vacation. I miss my kids and my bed. Conversations about what if's creep up, but I can't even go there. There was no way that my son was going through this for nothing.

Wednesday, January 07, 2009

After the scan's the other day, Lennon was all right at first. However, his insides are upset and if that isn't enough, there's another infection and an inflammation of his pancreas. So many reasons for his discomfort and no idea which one to treat first.

If all of this isn't enough, Lennon's strength and muscle tone are deteriorating. In my opinion, physical therapy should be in here working with him daily. I think if Lennon begins to work his muscles and has body movement, it will help his progress to heal.

Doctors agree that Lennon needs to be mobile so that his body can naturally absorb fluid. I asked why physical therapy wasn't working with him and no one was really sure why. We are helping him sit up because he can't do it on his own, but with consistency he will improve. Yet, no matter the treatment they included, Lennon was either peeing too much or not enough. His body needed the electrolytes but it didn't need all the fluid retention.

Sunday, January 11, 2009

Lennon is back on the breathing tube because of an upcoming CT scan and picc line placement. I hate that damn machine. The longer he is on the breathing tube, the more he will take to recover. He is however comfortable as I look at the numbers on his monitor. Damn that fluid.

A realty check with the doctor was not giving me much hope.

The doctor came to me and expressed that he and everyone else is extremely concerned. We do not know if he will come out of this alive.

My heart hurts.
The quick answer is that no one knows where the fluid is coming from, and on one knows what his body is doing. There are many other possibilities like a leak in the bile duct, or was it the clot in the portal vein? Or was this something completely different?

I have to believe that he will walk out of here. He's fought for 5 ½ years, why on earth would he quit now? Why would the universe put him through this and then simply let go? Death is not acceptable.

A difficult balance of reality and hope!

According to the transplant team, his portal vein is 100%

clotted and another vein, the name escapes me is partially clotted. Ok, how do we fix this?

They are not sure! Some procedures don't seem plausible and others are too risky.

I'll guess I'll be on pins on needles until then.

Friday, January 16, 2009

Here's the latest scoop of things.

As you know Lennon is having extensive fluid excess. He had some scans done in hopes to come up with an idea on how to move forward with all the clotting issues. He's not strong enough to undergo surgery that would allow them to go in and remove the clots.

After 8 hours, they shared with us that they could go in to balloon the portal vein to create a better flow for the blood to the liver, which then in turn would also help the body absorb fluid. The fluid excess is a reaction to parts of his system not working at a 100%.

If this is not successful, Lennon could be in the hospital for a long time until his body takes care of things naturally or he is strong enough for surgery.

It's been two months since the transplant and no home in

sight. I focus on my studies and doodle to seek refuge. It's helpful if my mind can focus on reality and escape it for just a moment.

Tuesday, January 20, 2009

Lennon is better since the ballooning of the vein, even though he is still on the breathing tube. His X-Ray improved daily but the puffiness remained.

Lennon is awake with less sedation and he will respond to questions with a nod or a shake of his head. He's quite calm with the breathing tube still in its place. Here's the crazy part, he's on three different sedation medications and shouldn't be awake.
His belly has gone down by 4 cm since yesterday. At one point his belly measured 76 cm. The fluid is again infected with a rare bug that no one has information about; including the infections disease department was unsure on how to treat it.

I remind myself that this is Lennon.

Saturday, January 24, 2009

The breathing tube is out and now we are observing on how this will go, and for the moment he's okay. He was a wild man hen they took the tube out trying to jump out of bed. Live with determination.

Monday, January 26, 2009

Lennon is out of bed, and in a wheel chair!! He still has the nasal oxygen, but is doing well.

He opened two of his Christmas presents with eagerness. This morning he laughed, when I told Physical Therapy how he tried to scoot out of bed with the breathing tube in because he wanted to go walking.

He is perking up a bit more each day. I am happy about the progress he is making, but also cautious. I cross fingers and toes and hope there are no other bumps in the road.
He is sitting without support! And that is amazing for someone who has lain in bed for so long 2 months. Before long he will be up and running again. His terms, his times, Lennon Steps!

Wednesday, January 28, 2009

Lennon wanted a Popsicle - color green. His nurse went looking in the PICU freezer, in the freezers on the floor and not a Popsicle in sight. One hour later, Lennon received not only one - but two popsicles - on purple and one white.

Lennon is doing great, drinking water. He must do so slowly or he will become ill. He's playing, talking fighting and hating everything: He wants out of bed, he wants to watch cartoons and play video games.

He is calm, smiling and laughing. Calling me when he needs a hug. To say that he is doing great is by far an understatement. For someone who has been bedridden, he has control of his head and neck muscles. He is sitting up longer and longer. Standing is not an option, but it won't be long.

He will move to the regular floor and possibly transfer to KCRC for rehabilitation. I am still holding my breath. I am nervous that something is going to go wrong. I can't shake it expecting another relapse. I am holding my breath to see how far we will make it.

Friday, January 30, 2009

Lennon is out of Intensive Care!

We are currently waiting on a room but he is leaving the PICU. I am elated about his progress. We do have to get him to eat.

This is a good day. The staff at the PICU has been excellent in caring for Lennon. We have come to love them, be their friends and share life stories with them. They love Lennon.

Lennon is amazing with a shining personality. He has affected everybody in such positive ways. He is a miracle and keeps inspiring me each and every day.

Sunday, February 01, 2009

Today Lennon walked 10 feet, from the bed to the sink. He also had a bath today. Yesterday was asked if he wanted a bath, which is only his favorite thing to do. She only brought a tub that is meant to wash the head in, in bed. Lennon was so unhappy about it that today he was sitting in an tub.

I think he received comfort by something we take for granted. He's sleeping right now due to his exhaustion. Heck I was tired just watching him work.

Lennon is not interested in food. He eats about 3-4 teaspoons of applesauce. Lennon hasn't had real food in three months, and he's still receiving nutrition through his IV. Perhaps if given the chance, turning the TPN and Lipids off would increase his appetite.

It's good to see him just smile. It's good to see him demanding time with me rather than me do my homework.

Friday, February 06, 2009

Lennon has no interest in food, and so the doctors agree to turn of the TPN and Lipids. Hopefully this will encourage his body to create hunger.

On Wednesday, his oxygen numbers dropped again and his right side was filled with fluid. Another ultrasound also gave us less favorable news, his hepatic vein collapsed again. This will require them to go in, balloon it again and maybe even place a stent to keep it open. If this works and he improves, we are heading to KCRC for physical therapy.

He did start eat a little, moving from potato chips to some peaches!

Monday, February 09, 2009

Lennon had a tapping of the fluid collection, ballooning of his hepatic vein and he's doing well. They didn't put in the stent because his body is still growing and it could cause some problems later on.

He did manage 5 bites of cake with icing! He does have to start eating or he will have his NG placed again.

Tuesday, February 10, 2009

The word on the block is that the call is being made for Lennon to be transferred to Kluge for physical rehabilitation. He will require a feeding tube, so that he can be fed at night.

Friday, February 13, 2009

"I want to go walking," he said.
"Ok but we need to wait for your meds first", I replied.
"Oh, good idea" he said.

He is just awesome and funny. We are being transferred to KCRC for Physical Therapy. We are being discharged from the Hospital.

Wow.

I thought this day would never come. There were days I thought I never see him smile or have a conversation with him. Today, he's smiling and talking about his ride to KCRC.

We are working on transitioning to food, but it is so

tricky because we really don't know what he likes. In the past we were limited to the food we could have and it was easier to maneuver. Now we explore and introduce new foods hoping he will like it.

I was reminded that there are bumps in our future because of the narrowing of the hepatic vein, or possible rejection of the liver. It's easy to forget when things are going well.

Sunday, February 15, 2009

Rehab is a less restrictive environment. He's already been walking down the hall. He has access to a wheel chair and absolutely loves riding in it and for a change he's wearing regular clothes.

This schedule will be full with Speech, Physical Therapy, and Occupational Therapy and Therapeutic Recreation. His feeds will change to a more normal schedule and be evaluated on day-to-day bases, while offering real food three times a day.

Wednesday, February 18, 2009

There has been progress! Lennon walks steadier even though his balance is still off. His new love is a trike he's able to use during physical therapy. He just has a blast riding around in the unit. He enjoys school, and all the activities; he's even been outside during the warmer days.

His mood is improving and he seems happier. He's still shy and can appear less cooperative until he gets to know the person.

Eating is still a challenge and we are trying to identify the reasons.

1. He has been so conditioned not to eat food i.e. protein restriction
2. He had the breathing tube several times
3. He is not used to using his voice and continues to whisper
4. His taste buds may have changed
5. He developed an aversion to food due to vomiting from sickness and withdrawals

He has to build a new relationship with food, one that is pleasant and allows him to enjoy it, but also be nutritional.

When the doctors are pleased, he can go home. It's tough to get him to eat when he's being fed via the NG tube. We are also working out his medication schedule. He's taking 16 different medications throughout the day. He will hopefully be on less on them by the time he gets home, and on a morning, noon and evening schedule.

On a different note, his ADHD symptoms are less at the moment. He is less fidgety and doesn't bounce all over the place. I don't think it is gone completely. In part however, some of it related to the Urea Cycle Disorder. The transplant did more than just save his life, it gave him an opportunity to live a more normal life.
He will have challenges due to his developmental delay, but I am excited about it life.

As I write this, I fell hesitant to get too excited. Isn't that the silliest thing, but I want to believe that the worst is over.

Wednesday, February 25, 2009

I talked to the psychologist and voiced my concern about Lennon's well being. There's so much pressure on his nutritional intake and not much else. I walked away knowing that at least someone agreed with me: less worry about nutrition, more focus on fun. His body is no longer ravaged by sickness. He will learn that his hair will grow back, the scar is permanent, rehab is temporary and laughing is good.

Through the journey of blogging about his journey, people have asked wonderful questions such as why the focus on nutrition. There are standards that every child must meet, including weight and growth. Lennon is supposed to meet a certain nutritional values. The problem is that Lennon clearly has never been the norm. He always controlled his food intake, and it will take time and patience before the relationship with food is established.

The matter is everyone understands that Lennon's mental health has to take priority. He has been sick for five years and has had 25 hospitalizations. All he knows is how to be sick.

The goal will be that after March 15th, he may come home with or without NG tube.

Friday, February 27, 2009

Lennon was awake all day. I feel like the changes we made with the formula have made a difference. His nutritionist doesn't agree and is stuck on what a normal five year old should have. He continues to improve since no one is harping on him to eat, and thank you medical advances for supplements for when he's low on vitamin D, calcium and phosphate.

My partner did some math and prior to the transplant, he never drank his daily requirements in fluids (900 ml). He snacked all day long rather than have a strict schedule of when to eat. I trust Lennon he knows what he needs because kids know intuitively what their body requires. Trusting my intuition has been the key element when it comes to parent Lennon.

Lennon takes one step forward and new hurdles arrive. He's been complaining about his legs hurting, which could be related to the extensive therapies he's doing throughout the day.

Last night after he woke up, we played with his bouncy ball and Lennon shared a real laugh.
Oh so good this feeling better business.

Monday, March 02, 2009

Over the weekend, Lennon wasn't feeling well and had a fever. After some testing he came back positive for VRE still but no other infection. Resting and encouraging fluids will be on our agenda.

I am forever the thinker about how to improve and make things better. The therapies Lennon has are so simple they could be done at home. I cold check his vitals, take his temperature, observe him and engage with him. In fact, I believe that if he were in his home environment with his family, he would very much improve.
I know this is about Lennon, but frankly I am tired of not sleeping my bed. Being away from my life and to give me some credibility, my current job has me trained as a medication aide, thus I know the basics about administering medicine. Further, because of my work I am also CPR and First Aid certified.

The added benefit of being at home is that we don't wear the gowns necessary for contact precautions. Come to think of it, maybe my kids will learn to wash their hands now that they have a better reason to do so. He would have the opportunity to go outside, play in his room or just hang out in the living room.

Lennon's care will not falter simply because we would be at home. We may qualify for a Medicaid waiver in which we can have a skilled nurse come to the house. Our working hours allow us to be with Lennon around the clock just about. The feedings and the feeding schedules can be adjusted at home, via telephone, via e-mail and via doctor visit.

He's been chronically sick for such a long time it' going to be difficult to feel good in a hospital setting.
I have been super sensitive and today everyone seems overly concern. He was admitted Nov. 18th, and this is March 2nd.

I am pushing to go home.

Wednesday, March 04, 2009

In discussion with the medical team yesterday, if Lennon can tolerate his feed and gain weight, we are looking at taking Lennon home Friday. That will make it 108 days away from home.

The diuretics he has been on were stopped to help our transition, so hopefully urinating isn't going to be an issue. He still has a plural infusion on the right side, and X-Rays will continue to monitor its size. He will be provided with a wheel chair because his recovery is simply taking loner than anticipated.

We encouraging him to drink on his own because if not we will have to add water to his feeds. He will also have a wheelchair for the time being for when we go long distance (dr. appt., stores). Of course he won't need it in the house but longer walks and such would still be too much on him. His recovery is probably taking longer than everyone had anticipated, but then again who anticipated the last three months?

He has been assessed for skilled nursing care in the home to provide respite care as well as allow us to go to work and handle life.

Projecting into the future, Lennon may have a G-tube placed rather than continue with the NG tube. While this means another surgery, the benefit lies in that it will be on his abdomen and thus easier to manage.

***

Friday, March 06, 2009

Lennon is home!

We came home about 1:30 this afternoon and it seems in this short time his mood has already improved. He wanted to play video games but I asked Lennon to wait until his siblings were home from school. To change his focus he is now watching Max & Ruby, a funny cartoon with bunnies as the main characters. Ruby, the big sister takes care of her younger brother Max. Max does not speak and appears to always cause mischief when in reality he's solving a problem. I imagine that Lennon really connects with this cartoon.

As we are settling into our home, I am finalizing plans for my residency in St. Paul, MN. After such an extensive hospital stay, I must leave my boy for one week.

Today, I focus on being home. Tomorrow we celebrate Christmas.

Monday, March 16, 2009

When I returned from my residency, a complete different child named Lennon greeted me. He smiled.
And in the short hours that I have been back I have seen him drink and eat.

Home is still the best place to heal.

Tuesday, March 17, 2009

Lennon has acid reflux or perhaps too much air. We had to stop his feeds and are waiting for the doctor to make a treatment decision. They agreed that feeds should be turned offer some time but that we should encourage him to drink PediaSure or another form of nutritional drink. Lennon is stressed out and appears anxious about being sick.

The challenge that continues to be a presence in our or should I say his life is the C.Diff. We are supposed to monitor his urine output but while he still has this horrendous diarrhea this isn't going to happen.

He is munching up a storm, and although he isn't eating consecutive whole meals three times a day, he snacks all day long, which is good. Pickles and potato chips are still his favorite foods and tomato soup. We saw progress in where he is now acknowledging hunger and willing to do something about it.

Lennon continues to have a liking to pickles and potato chips and has recently shown more interest in tomato soup. There is progress in his likes and wants and communication.

One day at a time we are mending him back to health.

The family is also mending again. Our life focused so much on Lennon's situation, creating chaos in our home life.

High-stress situations don't always just on one person, they wear on a whole family.

Saturday, March 21, 2009

Lennon has been spitting up and vomiting again and he's hungry at the same time. He manages to eat 2-3 bites and take breaks between his feeds.

According to the Transplant there are several reasons for the vomiting.

He has a stomach bug
He is producing too much acid and needs a higher dose of his stomach medication
He has too much air, which makes him gassy and could cause spitting up. The NG tube as curled at the end and the feeds are going to the esophagus.
He has another infection

We took Lennon to the emergency room because in addition to the vomiting, his scrotum was bleeding and with Lennon's coagulation problems I wanted them to look at it. The doctors contributed the bleeding to the ongoing C.Diff situation and since the bleeding was isolated to one area, we were sent home.

Our nurse at home is awesome and having her with us has been the best. I was able to focus on schoolwork and even my business. We are adjusting to the life and perhaps it was easier then I had envisioned.

Lennon had blood work done and the results were less than exciting as he came up low on potassium and vitamin k. His bilirubin and white blood cell counts were high. Yet no one had an inkling of an idea why.

I was concerned about weight loss. He appears weaker and is choses not to walk. He takes a few steps at a time before he has to sit and rest.

Sunday, March 22, 2009

Lennon spit up and this time there was blood involved. Alarm bells went off and I called transplant, which directed us to bring him in.

When we arrived, Lennon was able to have some popsicles. They had to take labs twice, because the first set of numbers was completely out of whack and didn't make sense. No one knew what was going on and so the doctors were playing medical detectives, they ordered an ultrasound. They are contemplating a biopsy on his liver and gave him a dose of vitamin K to aide the risk of bleeding. Waiting on a bed on the floor.

I can tell you that Lennon is starving! It is very painful to watch and see when your baby is crying and telling you that his belly hurts. He was allowed food and snacked on pretzels, chips and some French Fries. He even nibbled on a hamburger.

Lennon tested positive for C.Diff, again and another dose of antibiotics was added.

The doctor wants to take the stent out of the hepatic vein, however the ultrasound showed there's been no change.

Lennon: "I want to go home."

This can only mean he's tired of being in the hospital. His chronic sickness is not gone but it is a step in the right direction.

Lennon fell asleep and I felt a sense of relief. My own body was tense with my stomach in knots.

Monday, March 23, 2009

I didn't know is that there was a stent placed during the transplant surgery in the bile duct, just where the stitches are to connect the old and the new. In most cases, the stent will fall out.

Stent removal is scheduled for Tuesday.

The hope is that when the stent comes out he will feel better and we can be attempting to go home this weekend.

Keeping on my toes, there's been a change in schedules and the stent removal will be on Thursday. I was told they are also going a study on his stomach and intestines.

Until tomorrow world!

Tuesday, March 24, 2009

The imaging technicians put a lot of contrast down his NG tube and it showed when we changed his diaper. The result is encouraging that there is no obstruction, but he's quite ill and his belly is again extended. His belly is oddly shaped and appears to be swollen.

I had not seen any doctor for a while and I had them

paged. The resident came to check him out and according to him; his stomach is a bit irritated from the contrast

I am concerned that this really is something different.

I also made another discovery, after the nurse printed the lab results. His ammonia was 82 on Sunday and then 61 today. On my agenda to figure out what is going on, I am going to find out if there is a correlating between him being sick and the ammonia.

He's ready to go home, but telling him to wait until the doctors feel ready is pointless.

I don't like being rude and I was upset when a nurse told him that if he at too much, he could get sick. Lennon who already has challenges with food did not need to hear that. All the work we have done could undo in those few words. I asked her to run by me if she wanted to be helpful. Yes, a bit controlling on my part but man common sense!

However, her words had no impact. He's been eating pretzels, yogurt, 2 cherry tomatoes, ranch dressing, French Fries and Pringles. The nutritionist told me to not offer junk food and that he would start eating. I get that his current diet choices are not ideal. I understand nutritional standards and daily requirements. She must not know Lennon.

Speech pathology agreed that he must be given time to chose his food. Time and again I am proven to listen to my instincts and stand my ground.

I have to wonder if people really read the chart and never really listen to the patient or caretaker. Any kind of care always needs to be about the person, not just medical welfare.
The past two years he was on a special formula that he didn't like, and he isn't going to drink anything that reminds him of that. I know what he needs, but nothing in the last 6 months happened on medical terms, but in Lennon Steps.
On a lighter not, Lennon's hair is growing in. He's gone from a white blonde headed kid to a dark blond kid. So odd.

Wednesday, March 25, 2009

My biggest pet peeve is that Nurses are not giving consideration to the parents in the room that are still parenting albeit being in a hospital.

Lennon receives a breakfast tray with the following instructions: You will get your chips after you eat the yogurt.

Apparently this morning's nurse thought it would be totally okay to have chips at 8.a.m.

Yes, I know that I am totally contradicting what I am said before. Which really only enforces that I think this whole food thing is insane.

Wednesday, March 25, 2009

The stent removal is tomorrow. The plan is to remove the stent via scope and then clean out whatever junk may have accumulated.

The doctors think that Lennon's problems are due to the stent in the bile duct, thus causing problems in the colon area. The assumption is that once the stent is removed, his issues will go away. Lennon's belly may support their thought, as his belly is swollen again.

The poor kid as a major case of diarrhea and looks s pitiful. He doesn't even lift his head anymore.

I am nervous about tomorrow about as nervous when he got the transplants.

Thursday, March 26, 2009

A late start to the procedure but Lennon doing well.

The stent was in the wrong spot then where it was supposed to be. The bile duct leaked into Lennon's system causing all of the sickness he's been dealing with.

What the freaking hell!

A new stent went in, this time in its proper place.

While Lennon was sedated the doctors replaces his NG tube. Good stuff, except they used an NG tube that was too short and the wrong material on his skin. Lennon is allergic to the adhesive and will get blisters that resemble 2nd degree burns. What a flopping mess this was.

He's settled in his bed watching SpongeBob and looked like he was going to sleep. Instead he looed at me and said:

"I'm going home!"

"I'm sorry buddy we are not going home yet.

"Yes we are".

Friday, March 27, 2009

His stomach has already reduced in size and hopefully continues to make progress. The transplant team recommended that Lennon received the G-tube with his continued belly and food issues. Although, at the moment he can't keep anything down again and receives nutrition from TPN again.

Saturday, March 28, 2009

The cultures from yesterday and Lennon has a fungal (yeast) infection. He is running a fever and is listless. He has been keeping his medications down but continues to burp a lot, a side effect from the stent procedure. This infection came up really fast. One minute he was feeling good and the next he was complaining about a bellyache. His heart rate is holding at 190 and he will be going to the PICU for monitoring.

Monday, March 30, 2009

Lennon's heart rate is improving and is now at 157, but his breathing is still very labored and he is in need of oxygen support. The X-rays showed no fluid around the lungs but hat there is another collection of fluid on his left side. They will need to go in and rain the fluid.

Lennon's white cell count is low and his level of bleeding has increased and the doctors are in consult with hematology.

He is feisty telling the nurses to leave him alone when they check on him.

Oh remember the yeast infection seems to be all over the port in his chest. This isn't the challenging part, but communication seems to be. They have to remove the port to help Lennon's recovery but imagine my surprised when the surgeon came in to get my consent thinking I already knew that it would happen today. Apparently, the PICU team was in rounds and not decided that they didn't have time to talk to me. Blah!

Thursday, April 02, 2009

Removing the old port went well and he now has an external tunneled port on his arm. They restarted his feeds and he has been tolerating this well. They also added some new medication to help bind the contents of his stomach to control his massive diarrhea.

As Lennon continues to struggle with food, we are looking more and more at the G-tube in about 2-4 weeks. The NG tube he currently has could damage his nose, throat and even his stomach in the long term, and frankly until the food issue is resolved he will need nutritional support, although he is a master at eating chips.

And if dealing with a yeast infection isn't enough, Lennon also has airspace lung disease. My understanding is that its not pneumonia but can act similar with its breathing issues, and once his yeast infection is healed, this too should be going away.

In the mean time, love goes on with work, school and supporting the kids at home.

Saturday, April 04, 2009

Lennon was moved to the regular floor, but within hours he started vomiting blood. He was fiving FFP to help the coagulation. The reasons for his bleeding are open for speculation and assumption.

His coagulation is not what it should be?
He is taking aspirin
Other/new infections no one is aware of

This morning Lennon had blood in his diaper and in his NG tube and he's heading back to the PICU. There are giving him medication to stop the bleeding but he will need to be observed very closely. If that doesn't stop the bleeding they will need to sedate him and use a scope to find the source.

How much more does Lennon need to go though? Isn't this enough already?

Everybody is wondering how I am holding up. I stay focused on activates that allow me to distract myself. I mean I didn't sign a choice contract at birth asking if I wanted this for my son, but the universe must have had a reason for giving me this amazing little human.

Sunday, April 05, 2009

The bleeding seems to have stopped, thank heavens. While I am relieved he is cranky that he can't have anything to eat or drink until tomorrow when the medication runs out to help the bleeding and to make sure the food isn't casing him to bleed again.

I'm breathing a little easier this morning. Yesterday was bad, scary and a day I never want to experience again. I don't have much else to say this morning. I am emotionally drained and its sinking in how close we may have come to losing him had they not been able to stop the bleeding. He continues the fight, and he does not bow down.

Tuesday, April 07, 2009

Lennon has varices along the esophagus varices which are abnormal and enlarged veins in the lower part of the esophagus. This happens when normal blood flow to the liver is obstructed by scar tissue in the liver or a clot. This is so not the news I wanted to hear.

He is sleeping for the minute but even in his sleep he will call or me. Last night it went something like this: mommy mommy ooh ooh hehehe mommy mommy ooh ooh... So odd.

His belly had gotten bigger again and another ultrasound hopefully would shed some light on what is happening. The liver is functioning okay but not too optimum. They aren't sure how much of his problems are related to the liver function and want to keep him in ICU because he may be brewing another infection. His x-rays were whited out today more than yesterday and he will be receiving another chest tube to help drain the fluid.

His breathing his labored and they doctors are worried. This too will pass and we will head towards recover. The alternative is not acceptable right? They are not giving him any antibiotics right now because sometimes less is more.

This seems all so eerily familiar.

I am not sure where my mind is at the moment. I have no

idea about the future and once again I wonder if we will make it home.

Wednesday, April 08, 2009

Yesterday, Lennon received another chest tube because he has fluid everywhere. Today they did a CT Scan and biopsy - though they are not suspecting a rejection issue – they are hoping to find some answers to Lennon's situation.

Part of me is scared to know and I have flashbacks from prior to diagnosis. It makes me angry to think that he has to go through so much just to be alive. The things we take for granted.

I realized part of me is numb. Four months ago, a chest tube was a huge deal, today not so much.

Crying is a healing emotion and anger is a motivational emotion, lessons learned in grad school. I cried. The flood gates opened to relief all this penned up emotion.

I went home and made soap before going back to the hospital because for just one minute I needed to focus on something else. For one minute I didn't want to think about all the possibilities. For one minute I didn't want to think at all, let alone feel anything. I miss Lennon, I miss him a lot and the transplant has changed him. But I feel his pain; I can see it in his face, how uncomfortable he was. He sets the example of what it means to fight for your life.

The nurses often tell me how much that little boy loves me, like when he says my name in his sleep or when his mental state is altered. He says my name to let me know he really needs me, to stroke his head and to tell him I love him. He says my name to make sure I didn't leave him.
My kids are amazing. They keep the house running, do their homework, feed the animals and don't set the house on fire. They are mini-adults. They too are my strength and inspiration.

This post has gone on longer than I intended but that happens. I feel more drained these days, so I will end this with saying good night and thanks for all your prayers and thoughts as Lennon continues his battle of recovery.

Thursday, April 09, 2009

The CT Scan showed that Lennon's colon; well his whole bowl system is inflamed. This develops fluid in areas where there doesn't need to be fluid. He is on four antibiotics. They are checking the kidney and pancreas function, and those appear to be well.

Lennon now has nodules on his lungs that could be either lymph nodes from the yeast infection. Lennon's body has several things going on medically but the challenge once again is what to treat first.

He is on the breathing tube because he is so incredible sick again that keeping him comfortable is most important. It's been another day of roller coaster emotions.

Friday, April 10, 2009

Prayers, positive energy and thoughts is what will get us through this time. Lennon is on the breathing tube being supported comfortably with sedation. And the hits just keep on hitting, Lennon has colitis and inflamed bowels.

The doctors are worried but tell me they are not given up hope. Their words!

This is very difficult time for us as we are not sure which way it will go.

Lennon is critically ill and only time can tell if he is going to pull through this one.

I hope, I pray, I cry, and I worry.

Sunday, April 12, 2009

Things are unchanged. He is comfortable and heavily sedated. He is a little puffball and they are going to help him lose the fluids. Talking with one of the doctors today, it could be this yeast infection that caused all the trouble. He is very sick.

Knowing that he has pulled through in the past it is difficult thinking about the alternatives. I have a lot of anxiety that leaves me with chest pain. Self-care is not something I am good at. The nurses have encouraged me to leave, to go rest and it is so hard to do.

The doctors can only do so much and hat the rest is up to Lennon and the powers that be. It is difficult to fathom that after the long fight, it could just end. I believe in his spirit and his will to live.

We fear the unknown! How true those words are today and every day. The doctors do everything they medically can but in the end it may not be enough.

Monday, April 13, 2009

Lennon is on diuretics again, which has helped lower the vent settings. Small progress is good.

An ultrasound showed that Lennon has several pockets of fluid. The chest tube can't reach them and so they may have to go in and drain the bubbles themselves. They will do a bronchial procedure to get a specimen of Lennon's lungs. Hopefully it will give an answer about the nodules.

Everyone's positive thoughts, energy and prayers are appreciated. Some minutes are easier than others. I still try to keep busy as to not get overwhelmed and too concerned, but sometimes a song, a word, a commercial will bring to reality how sick my little boy really is, and how much I miss him.

Wednesday, April 15, 2009

Nothing really going on today after the procedure he is resting comfortably.

There are many things that are running through my mind. Was it the stent from the procedure? Is it the C.Diff that doesn't want to go away? Is it the bile duct leak? Is it the liver even though the biopsy came back ok? Are his lungs or rather the right lung his problem for the issues? Is it the yeast infection, and the fact that it was attached to his port? There are so many questions to where there seem to be no answer to. That's tough.

Saturday, April 18, 2009

This is my 100st post about Lennon and his health and things are unchanged. His sedation is troublesome as his blood pressure wants to bottom out and his heart rate wants to do similar stuff.

His X-Rays are playing tricks on us, one morning he looks fine and the next day they are horrible again. His chest tube needed some clot busting medication to get it going again, which helped the X-Rays to look better.

We don't know how long he will be on the ventilator because the fluid is still there; the belly is still big but still no real answers as to why.

There really isn't much else to say right now, except we sit with Lennon, watch his monitor, missing him and hoping that we get to interact with him soon.

Friday, April 24, 2009

I haven't posted in awhile because well there hadn't been any changes. Today we have progress.

Lennon looks skinny, as most of the fluid has gone. He is more awake as they changed his sedation levels. The doctors also learned from the last time and proceeded to be on top of any withdrawals he may be experiencing.

His belly was at 65.5 cm yesterday but this morning he's back at 68 cm. He ahs not gone to the bathroom for some time and may need laxative support. One moment he has diarrhea and the next moment nothing.

I have been trying to stay busy as this waiting is driving me crazy. I am going home every other night to see the kids and sleep in my bed. The world doesn't stop when one is sick.

I pondered about how much he means to us, me, his brothers, to everyone. How energetic he is, how busy he can keep us, how funny he is. His disorder and his disabilities have not impacted his spirit. He keeps fighting, from somewhere within that I admire. People, who are complete strangers to us, have given us support, a gentle reminder on his impact on so many lives.

Wednesday, April 29, 2009

Lennon is still on the breathing tube. The C.Diff had waxed and waned. These days, his vent settings are lower, his belly size remains stable, and his feeds have started again. When Lennon is on his right side (the problem lung) Lennon's heart rate and blood pressure. They gave clot-buster medication through the chest tube, and he put out almost a liter of fluids and required a blood transfusion. They are now using clot-buster medication every twelve hours to keep the chest tube clean and able to remove fluids. It's up to Lennon, if he progresses he cold be off the breathing tube by Friday.

Lennon does what Lennon wants, when Lennon wants it and we call them Lennon Steps.

Thursday, April 30, 2009

Lennon was taken off the breathing tube at 2:30 p.m. this afternoon. He still needs oxygen assistance, periodic suction of fluids and coughing. He is resting with the help of some sedation. He looks comfortable. Just before sedation, he was fighting and attempting cry and yell, like the Lennon we love and know!

Tuesday, May 05, 2009

It's been less than a week since the breathing tube came out. He is sitting up for extended periods of time, poking fun at people. He is dealing with withdrawals, but he sure looks good! He is watching TV and wants to go walking! For someone who has been down without any mobile activity, he is amazing. The doctors have deemed him unbelievable, but in a good way! He is allowed to drink, but food is still being held back.

Today Physical Therapy will come and work with him and then the schoolteacher will be by later. That is if he's not sleeping!

We played the stretch our limbs game and he had a blast, even if it was for only a few minutes. Last night, he was not able to drink anything but could do swaps with water to "rinse" his mouth. I explained to him he had to wait, his response: "Watch your mouth". Typical Lennon.

They are not sure what it will take for him to go home. His breathing should be without oxygen requirement, and he should be holding his food.

Lennon steps!

Thursday, May 07, 2009

Lennon has received official orders to get out of ICU and go the floor!

One of the chest tubes will come out today, and the other will be evaluated. He is sleeping. I am cautious about everything at the moment, and working towards getting things together to home school. I often just want to wrap him in a bubble of protection. I am not sure what the next steps are. But for now I am happy and excited that he is doing so much better.

Saturday, May 09, 2009

For Lennon to eat a handful of chips! This is literally what the orders say! Lennon has moved from the PICU to the floor.

The plan is for Gastro, Nutrition and Speech to get together and create a plan to get him eating. Currently he is on continuous feeds 25ml/hour. They will look at the calorie intake he needs to receive and ensure that his intestines can handle it all. Speech can help in being playful with the food, encouraging him to eat.

The question is when are we going home? Will he receive a g-tube prior to going home? Or will they place the G-tube when they remove the stent that will need to come out in a few weeks?

Lennon is doing really well. He is the boy I knew 6 months ago. He is funny, laughing, playing and being goofy. He wasn't quite like that when we left Kluge. He appeared more depressed than. Now he doesn't seem so depressed.

Today when one of the nurses asked him:" Are you better now?"

Lennon said: "Not yet".

Funny Dude!

He gets tired out easily, and breathing is not 100% but improving. Being able to get out of bed is helping this time around.

Wednesday, May 13, 2009

The doctors want to make sure that he can hold his feeds without vomiting because just yesterday he spend a day of being ill because his clonidine patch fell off and it took us some time to figure that out. Have mercy!

Lennon is still positive with C.Diff, and the doctors are communicating with infections disease to approve probiotics to his diet.

Lennon just called me on the phone to let me know: "Mom I walked".

What an amazing kid he is. He has such motivation and courage to not only live, but also to overcome anything and everything. I am in awe of his spirit.

I suspect that the bile duct leak had a lot to do with him feeling like crap. He is laughing, playing, dancing in the bed, and using his muscles by stretching and pretending to run from a bear.

Wednesday, May 20, 2009

C.Diff, is a persistent bug. My intuition tells me that the longer he is in the hospital it will be tougher to fight it.

The doctors will have to do some number crunching and observe how he handles the feeds.

He is doing really well these days. He is walking half way down the hallways. He's sitting up and watching his cartoons well SpongeBob. I feel that some of Lennon's behavior is back to baseline, meaning he is feeling really good.

Sunday, May 24, 2009

Let me just say that Lennon is doing AWESOME, despite the C.Diff! The last week he has been weaned of the TPN and lipids and they added pedialyte to his nutrition intake to avoid dehydration. He has been tolerating his feeds, which are now 80ml/hour for 14 hours to a total for 600 ml of his feeds, and 300 of water.

His personality and activity level are back. He is favoring one of his feet, something to keep my eye on. Initially they didn't want us to go home until Tuesday. The hospital and I played medical vs parental opinion. I feel that from the bottom of my heart that he needs to go home! Call it mother's intuition.

He will do He will do much better at home! I think that he will start eating, give him a chance.

Thanks for all the prayers, positive energy and thoughts that have come our way. There aren't enough words to show my gratitude to all of you! Please stay tuned, as we will continue to update the blog about our ups and downs, progresses and setbacks, though we hope that the setbacks are nothing like what we have experienced since November 2008!

We're home!

Friday, May 29, 2009

We are working on getting all of his appointments set up, medication and tube feedings. The hospital and insurance company are working on getting the nursing care.

Encouraging him to walk though he is dealing with a

problematic heel right now. He is complaining about his legs and feet hurting quite a bit so we are letting him taking it easy.

Saturday, June 06, 2009

Tomorrow it will be two weeks since he came home. We have to visit Gastro once a week, and OT/PT come to the house to work with Lennon. He will receive a few hours a day for four weeks throughout the summer and join his ranks on the first day of school.

But how is Lennon doing, you ask? I think he's doing well and continues to improve but some things are very clear.

His food issues/aversion is going to take a long time ~ say a year or better
We constantly worry that the ND tube will come out

The doctors are creating a plan on tackling two procedures at one time. He will be receiving the G-tube and they will remove the stent from his bile duct.

Lennon's belly continues to be extended but it doesn't bother him. In the morning he a watches cartoon and follows people around the house. By the afternoon however, he is stiff and complaining about leg pain and he continues on, determined to walk through the house.

Lennon at home is beautiful, funny and witty. Lennon in public not so much. Lennon these days is shying away from adults and other kids; even people he knew. I try not to dwell on this so much, keeping in mind what he has been. Overall the consensus is that everyone is happy that he's home.

Friday, June 12, 2009

Lennon will have surgery on Monday to have his g-tube placed and we be will be at hotel hospital for about 1-3 days. Today we are going to have a CT-Scan to decide if this will be invasive or with a scope.

Lennon is faring well. His food and hunger issues are quite the struggle and with a family of size, food money is limited.
We spend a lot of time preparing food he's chosen just to watch him not eat it.

Monday, June 15, 2009

The G-tube placement went well and Lennon is very unhappy about the tube in his belly and was very concerned where his other tube (the one stuck to his face) was. He had a hard time understanding that this new tube in the belly will do the same thing.

The next two months we will have to be diligent to keep up with him, and the tube.

I am not sure what I was expecting but a tube hanging off 12 inches was not it. The care he requires for the next two months is going to be incredibly big. The tube hangs out about 12 inches from his belly. Once it is healed up i.e. the skin around his tube, the doctor will reevaluate to see if they can shorten it for mere cosmetic purposes and that it is not dangling from his belly. We're going to need to find a way to secure it so he can run around.

Wednesday, June 17, 2009

Lennon is doing well. After the procedure there appeared to be a kink in the tube on the inside that they had to fix. Overnight they ran pedialyte in 10 ml increments every two hours and by this morning he was back to the 'normal' rate of 80-mls/an hour. In about an hour or so we will be going home.

During Lennon's illness my eldest grew up. He will be 17. Geez, it was just yesterday I changed his diaper so it seems. He opted not to go to King's Dominion, instead we are fishing.

Lennon settled in very quietly tonight. At 7 p.m. he was ready for bed but due to his medication schedule we made him wait till 8 p.m. He is very good and I think he "gets" the tube thing and is able to tell me if he's in pain. So here is to sweet dreams Lennon.

Wednesday, June 24, 2009

Lennon is 6 today. I cried. I remember when he first came home how cute he was. How challenging he was to take care of. When he started to get his teeth and walk that all he wanted was chips and hot dogs. How many times a day and night I would walk in or wake up to him being so sick and unresponsive. I remember telling the doctors that there is something wrong but all they could tell me is that he was dehydrated.

I remember the days when I could not understand a word that he said. The day of his diagnosis feels like it was just yesterday, the fear, the worry the unknown future. I remember the struggle to get him to take his medications and his "special" ice cream (his formula) and all the things he could not eat.
I remember the day of the discussion of the transplant recognition what a miracle he is. I even appreciate the hysterics he goes through when he is in pain. I smile when I think about him running when he still is challenged to walk without falling. I love how he

demands his attention, even if it is inconvenient for everyone else. I love that he says the funniest things, that he likes food fights and that he is full of love and life.

Thank you!

Friday, June 26, 2009

Lennon was back in the emergency room with a fever of a103 and labored breathing. They did blood cultures and within 8-10 hours have grown some bacteria. The infection is related to his port. Of course this means they will have to take his port out. We could be here for a few days to get the infection under control.

Tuesday, June 30, 2009

So the gram-positive infection turned out to be an e-coli infection in his tunneled central line. They are currently treating it with antibiotics. If nothing re-grows in his cultures and he can get off the oxygen, we could possibly look at going home Thursday or Friday. This means he could ride in the fire truck during the parade on the 4th of July in Scottsville.

Thursday, July 02, 2009

Lennon is home and feeling better. We are giving him antibiotics through his IV line. I am happy though because on Saturday, Lennon gets to ride in a Fire truck in the 4th of July Parade in Scottsville. How neat is that? I hope he likes it and has an awesome time.

Saturday, July 04, 2009

And his ride in the fire truck. The local Scottsville Fire Company gave Lennon a
Genuine Firefighter hat with his Name on it as well as a T-Shirt.

Wednesday, July 08, 2009

Lennon seems to be coming down with a cold. He is still not very active and we are certainly not pressuring him to do anymore than he wants to or can.

Lennon continues to go through a lot of food as if his mind can't make up what he really wants. He chooses some foods he liked before the transplant such as oatmeal but is also venturing out to foods he could not have before like cereal with milk. It is very slow progress in his recovery. He seems very young at times indicating that his development suffered throughout his disease and he "requires" a lot of mom attention and is rarely satisfied with anyone else comforting him. He did become physical and I can't figure out if it is because he is not feeling well or whether it is that he is not getting his way. This stuff is so hard to figure out.

Sunday, July 12, 2009

Lennon was very excited about his party until it happened. We sat up the yard with tent and decorations. We talked about kids coming over, his daddy being there and of course presents!

Once people arrived, Lennon became a little shy. I think he gets overwhelmed when lots of people have paying attention to him. We filled water balloons and his brother showed him what to do. It was like the sky lit up, his face carried the biggest smile and his party turned into the best water balloon fight ever. Lennon was tired but he expressed he had an awesome party.

Thursday, July 23, 2009

Lennon's steps!

Lennon is getting around more, but his nights are filled with constant tossing and turning. We know that Lennon has insomnia and that part of his brain was damaged from too much ammonia when the disorder still riddled his body. He is also adjusting to sleeping with a tube out of his belly.

***

I reflect every day how close we have come to losing him and how sad and heartbreaking the days were and how supportive everyone has been. Those are days I simply cannot forget but I cherish every day in which he smiles, is funny and shows his not so favorable sides. I see the delays in his development but we have found ways to embrace them. For some time I felt angry on why this little guy had to go through all of this, but if he hadn't it would be Lennon. The strength, courage and his carefree attitude towards everything are awesome.

Lennon is very engaging and every one that seems to meet him is merely taking back by his wonderful personality. He grows into everyone's heart effortlessly. Lennon is still dealing with ascites, thrombosis with veins, coagulation issues and nutritional problems. He currently his Vitamin D deficient and requires additional supplements for phosphorus and potassium.

Wednesday, August 05, 2009

Screams and tears and no sleep plagued the Lennon. We called the doctor who stated to keep it clean and dry - Done! Over the weekend however, the area became red and another phone call to the doctor, bring him in on Monday!! It was not infected but out of precaution Lennon is on an antibiotic. They even marked the area for us to observe and let them know if the area changes in size.

In other news, Lennon grew 3 inches since June and he gained 700 grams, weighing now 42.5 lbs.

Lennon had his annual eye appointment. He did amazingly well - cooperated most of the time.

The result: Lennon will need glasses at some point as his near-sightedness will get worse over time. The doctor did not want to move forward with getting classes now due to Lennon's development.
Lennon is cranky, which means he is no kind of fun. He was up until midnight and up again by 7 a.m. It is time for an appointment with Neurodevelopment to address sleep and behavioral issues. He is using the bathroom mostly in the mornings, he is trying.

Tuesday, August 11, 2009

Lennon has a hard time with time; he understands day from night (light and dark) but how many minutes or hours something is kind of eludes him. The worries and stress has changed (some), but I am learning to relax more and allow myself to daydream and dabble in my creativity that I call "Hippie's Creations", a way to sell my crochet and pyrography art and support the family.

However, these past days I found myself reflecting on the experiences, on the emotional roller coaster, the physical wear & tear, the strain on our family and the strength that we individually and as a family unit exuberate. It goes without saying almost that I admire each and every person in my immediate family. My children who never indicated jealousy, who were at all times genuinely concerned not only about Lennon, but also me. With many of parental frustrations as our live has turned (semi) normal; I am in awe of them. It is an amazing feeling to know that your children can live without you when the time comes, though has a parent you hope they always stay close and they may always need you in some capacity.

Lennon's siblings are back in school and Lennon is disappointed. He loves school, he loves to play with his friends, sing songs and have circle time. I feel sad for him but I do not feel guilty for keeping him at home.

I wonder if he gets lonely, I wonder because he doesn't say he is? He does tell me occasionally that he's bored. Lennon has never truly learned how to play; it is something he is just now learning to do. It is now time for Lennon to develop play.

Sometimes I am challenged to recognize that he is 6 years old physically and he is developmentally delayed. We don't know if he will ever catch up developmentally. Lennon's future is not bleak. There are opportunities that allow him to live a happy, fulfilled and successful live, which is really a mother wants for her children.

The blog is never intended to strip me naked in my emotions; it is however an open window into our live.

Thursday, August 13, 2009

On this day two years, Lennon was diagnosed with Urea Cycle Disorder and as I think about that day, we are in the hospital once again. Lennon has been running a low-grade fever (99.0 - 100), vomited and complained about his belly hurting. He appears to be working on an infection. The issue is we don't know if the infection is around the tube or if it is a central line, but the doctor is clearly worried about a line infection.

Wednesday, August 19, 2009

Another infection in the line. I have been quite busy and am just now getting to the update. We spend the weekend at the hospital and went home Monday with IV medication to treat the line infection. Lennon's central line will be coming out on Friday in a clinic visit with anesthesia procedure and hopefully we will not encounter any more infections.

Add to his plight, Lennon's C.Diff flared up again more than ever.

When will this end?

Thursday, September 17, 2009

I still find myself wondering about the ammonia in his system. So I have been staying away not because I didn't want to write. We did an overnighter at the hospital just to make sure that he wasn't developing anything again.

He has overcome the cold fairly well. We are down to visiting he doctor once a week and receives academic instructions for 30 minutes a day.

Progress is amazing!

Can I just tell you that I have heard about the old Lennon I know from pre-transplant? His nurse took him to the store, and according to her he was very hyper, not listening, unable to stop himself, knocking things off the shelf. After they came home, he was hanging from the freezer door, disappearing into the front or the backyard and just go. My heart sank because his behavior was very much like when the ammonia was the main cause.

I don't think his ammonia is up, but we are planning a trip into town tomorrow to check his bleeding level and we might throw ammonia in as well. I am wondering however if perhaps yesterday was the first day in a really long time that he maybe has felt really good? I don't know that I can say how he feels and when he feels good or awesome. I can tell you when he's okay or not so well, but knowing when he feels absolutely good.

I don't know if yesterday was a fluke. I was told that if he's like that, that I am a strong woman. In my world, Lennon was like that for a really long time, uncontrollable, violent, unable to stop, not able to think and acknowledge the risks. This is how I know Lennon; maybe his personality just took an extensive vacation after the transplant. I don't know his behavior will always be a challenge I think.

His favorite past time is playing the PlayStation. We are getting into a routine with a visual schedule. We have allowed Lennon to relax and take it easy. Now that he appears to be home, he too must learn the rules.

Friday, September 18, 2009

Me: Are you ready for bed?
Lennon: Maybe
Me: What does that mean?
Lennon: that's English mom!

Me: Are you ready for bed?
Lennon: In four minutes
Me: In four minutes?
Lennon: that's what I said

Sunday, October 04, 2009

Now that Lennon is doing well, I find that I am less blogging, as we are busy with normal life! This is good but doesn't mean life isn't still challenging and instilled with worries and fears. We note there are good days and bad days when it comes to his mood and behavior. The other day as I was getting ready for an event to sell my creations and Lennon and I went shopping. I recall the days where I was resistant to take him with me because of the behavioral or vomiting. These days however, hanging out with Lennon is charming, fun.

He shares his thoughts, sings songs, and is amazed by the items one can find at the store. As we were walking through the aisles, he exclaimed: "Wow mom this stuff is fancy". He helps pushing the cart, he wants to stand on the cart, he wants to touch everything and take everything in.

Lennon still struggles with coagulation issues in; we still watch for bruising; checking his temperature, blood pressure. We can see the flower blossoming that has waited to grow for so long. Lennon looks forward to his physical therapy and his schoolteachers. The thirst of knowledge in him has emerged. The hungry caterpillar currently is his favorite book and he can tell you the story from beginning to end. When he is done learning or working, he will proclaim: I AM DONE. When the teachers do not acknowledge this the first time: I AM DONE I SAID.

I live in the small town and I am in awe of people and grateful to our friends. What our family has endured is no small feat. We don't complain and yet we constantly hear: I don't know how you all do it. We do what needs to be done.

Monday, October 12, 2009

Today we are heading to the Blue Ridge Parkway for some hiking. Lennon used to really enjoy that until his ammonia had gotten the better of him. It seems like forever since we were able to do things as a family.

Wednesday, October 28, 2009

Lennon is doing remarkably well, spoiled to the core. He is gentle, loving, kind, and considerate. He is also manipulative, moody, demanding. He's matured on some levels which is positive, but clearly in some areas he's lacking the 6 year old knowledge, and those are the things I fear will not recover or it will be a long time.

It is nice to have the ability to worry less and just when I count my blessings, he coughed and I was worried he'd choke on a blood clot. It is nerve' wrecking sometimes because just when you think, yes we are ok, nope something creeps up to let you know to be on guard.

Lennon goes to bed at 8, however he often is still up until 10 p.m. or midnight, or later. His insomnia is keeping his brother awake who must get sleep for school. It's still tough at time, but I am happy to say they are better.

Thursday, November 12, 2009

Life with Lennon means knowing a sleeping disorder, dealing with behaviors challenges and mood swings. We changed from the clonidine patch and changed to the clonidine pill and he became all out of sorts. He was out of it and just simply not himself. His speech was out of sorts and his vision appeared impaired. My intuition thought that it was related to the clonidine pill and once we made changes with his doctor to something less sedating, he was much improved.

I had a meeting with his school for his eligibility meeting and discussing how to get him back into the school. We decided that he should attend part-time until after the winter break. School is so important due to him being so behind but more importantly, he would be less bored sitting around at home.

Tuesday, November 17, 2009

A moment of reflection, tomorrow is the first year anniversary of his liver transplants. I tell you it's been a crazy year. Life is too short not to follow your heart and pursue your dreams. Lennon has taught some amazing lessons despite the pain.
Lennon is the icon for having a will to live. He fought and his spirit was stronger. I hear that he has this strength from me, because of my childhood in foster care. His story is more remarkable to me.

Lennon's diagnosis has encouraged me to pursue my dream to be a counselor and help children and adolescents. In 9 months I will have my master's degree.

He is a constant reminder to stay true to yourself and true to your heart.

Nothing is impossible and everything can be overcome. I know that I must find closure and when the time is right I will heal.

Lennon steps, we call them Lennon steps

Thursday, December 10, 2009

These past few weeks, I saw a kid who struggled to learn but who doesn't quit. Despite the fact that he is behind his peers, and that it is harder for him to retain the material, he just doesn't waver. The brain is so tricky sometimes because some material he retains easily, while other subjects he just cannot for the life of him remember what he's learned the day before. My only hope is that as he is healing, so will his brain.

Today is the second day of school for Lennon since November 18th, 2008. I want to cocoon him in a bubble. Lennon is well even though he tires easily, despite it he can hardly contain his excitement for school. He is smiling ear to ear and is ready to get the show on the road. It is amazing how much he actually wants to learn, if only more children had his thirst for knowledge.

Lennon is eating more these days like pickles, chips, oranges, sometimes rice, cheese, sometimes peanut butter and jelly and sometimes oatmeal or cereal. We know he can eat, the challenge is simply to do more substantial meals but this is really easier said than done. I don't understand what is blocking him from eating food, unless this entire ordeals may have been too much to handle.

Part Four

Monday, January 25, 2010

Lennon is singing and dancing. It is hard to fathom that there could be something seriously wrong when he looks good and behaves normal.

He just mooned me!

This morning we were told that test results would not be in for another week. You guessed it, we are in the hospital because Lennon's ammonia went too a 100. The doctors are frazzled but suspect that the clotting of his veins is the root of his current problem. While the ascites has gone down, his veins and vessels are more prominent. When looking at his body, its like you are looking at a map of water roads.

So far today, he has made belly flops, attempted to fall of

the bed and ran around his hospital room. I'd say he's feeling all right.

Thanks for staying tuned to "as Lennon turns the world".

Friday, January 29, 2010

Lennon made it home Monday afternoon, and I have been playing catch up with school and work. One of the test results that are finally back is his Epstein Barr Virus number that rocketed to 2300. This causes a huge concern with the ammonia going up, which is now at a steady 75. The doctor is worried that he has post-transplant lymphoproliferative disease (PTLD), a complication of solid organ transplant.

We were sent home and wait for further test results to come in. Lennon requires a lot more care because of turning blue.

Saturday, January 30, 2010

We got a phone call to make changes to some of his medication dosage but if this doesn't help the Epstein Barr Virus numbers, he may be looking at a biopsy to check the liver.

Devastatingly enough however we were told that he may need another liver transplant in about a year – give or take his health.

Another liver transplant?

Here we are maintaining with medication via IV at home, change in his diet and feeds and the amount he needs to drink. Watching carefully for lethargy and behavior changes. Keep an eye on any lymph-node developments and watching him slowly master milestones typical for younger children. His speech still delayed and his emotional stage still much that of a 3 or 4 year old, he put his own pants on.

Monday February 15, 2010

No concrete results of what is going on with the liver. I know that the EPV (Epstein Barr Virus) numbers are scarily elevated.

Yesterday he made me several valentines while I was lying down on the couch. Once I got up, he said, "Mom, you forget to make my valentine". So we sat down together and I created his valentine.

Thursday, February 18, 2010

Lennon had his weekly appointment today and he has chronic liver disease. The clot in the portal vein, the collapse of the hepatic vein and the clot in the vena cava do not allow enough blood flow to the liver. He's at risk for developing more clots, experiencing liver failure and that there is a good chance he will have another transplant.

For now he is well. He's protein restricted again until further notice. The IV medication will be changed to oral so that he can return to school. Of course, if he cannot handle being in school he will return to homebound education. Clearly, the doctor's don't want him on the monkey bars, but he's still a boy. At this point, we are living with quality over quantity.

Lennon is a little moody today, but we are allowed a day where we are not on our top game.

It is quite apparent that his road of medical turmoil is not over and that more complications are. There are many facets of Lennon's care that cannot be predicted or speculated on.

The doctors are keeping a close eye on him, the nursing staff is taking care of him, and we at home watch him closely, paying attention to every mood swing, behavioral episode and the hyperactivity if it elevates.

I have never nor will I ever turn down any prayers, positive energy or anything else that is beneficial in our journey and foremost in Lennon's journey. I will continue to write posts about the good days and the bad days. There will be days and weeks perhaps of silence, but know that in the day of silence it is then when we experience normalcy.

Wednesday, February 24, 2010

My emotions and my stress level are filled to capacity. I am on edge about the next second, and am living with a constant headache.

Stupid cut on his finger! It really shouldn't be this dramatic, except that Lennon still has coagulation trouble. We bandaged the finger and didn't give it another thought except when we took the Band-Aid off, we also took off the clot that had developed and he started bleeding again.

He is a little tired today, took a nap and perked right up. I am used to him being emotional to get his way or because he isn't feeling good, but one of our dogs got off his chain overnight and was hit by a car. In dealing with the aftermath looking for Draco and finding him in a ditch was hard enough. Having to explain it to the kids so much harder. I was talking to Lennon's brother Jarod and

Lennon asked what had happened. I told him that Draco got hit by a car and died, and this might sound harsh but I just couldn't sugar coat this one.

Lennon yelled: "That's not fair, he's never coming back" and with that buried his head into his blanket.

I still have a difficult time putting into words how this affected me. He loved that dog. At any time he would be in the backyard playing with all three dogs. He literally watched him grow from puppy stage to big dog. It is a sad day in our home.

Wednesday, March 17, 2010

Tonight, I was painfully reminded that I am human. I don't have it all together. Lennon was crying out from his room that his belly hurt, and one look at the feeding pump, I noted that I didn't change the feeding rate.

It's amazing how devastating something like this can feel. It wasn't the end of the world and the mess was easy to clean up, but it doesn't change the fact I didn't pay attention.

The other one of my kids told me I need to do a better job watching Lennon, so that Lennon doesn't go into his room. Ugh.

Are you serious?

Sometimes it's all too much to bear and I wonder how much more of this I could handle.

If all of this isn't enough, the school is also giving me grief. The challenge is that if we allow his private duty nurse to be with him, the school will do very little to save him, should he need it. This is what I was told anyways. After some frustrating phone calls to the nursing company, the bottom line is that if a private duty nurse goes to school with Lennon, the school doesn't get paid.

Money, money is always the issue.
We are now without a nurse on Friday. Lennon is returning to school Thursday.

I try to keep things together. I try to make sure that all kids have attention. I try to make sure my relationship has attention. I try to keep my business going. I try to manage my internship. I try to stay on top of my schoolwork. Tonight I just don't have it together!

Sunday March, 2010

Lennon's EBV levels are through the roof and he needs a CT Scan to check for lymph nodes. I can't help but wonder what the CT scans showed and if we have to worry about a Lymphoproliferative Disorder. I can only hope and pray this isn't the case because Lymphoproliferative disorders are among the most serious and potentially fatal complications of chronic immunosuppression in organ transplant recipients.

What in the world?

Again we find ourselves in limbo about diagnosis and prognosis. I am trying to maintain calm, collected and 'just wait for the results' and hope for the best. I suppose I can't really elaborate on much more until I know 'something'.

Wednesday April 7, 2010

Lennon and his brothers went to their dad's house!!! This is good and challenging for me because it gives a lot of room for thought that I don't usually have much time for. I am humbled and often reminded about how lucky he is and how inspiring he can be.

Lennon is enjoying school though he doesn't talk too much about it. He is still very focused on his video games and the newest fascination, army dudes. He's still also focused on death and dying. I don't know how to approach this subject. Do I leave it alone?

The severity of our reality eludes my six year old.

Tuesday April 20, 2010

Lennon is so funny and I wish I could share videos of him of the things he does and says. He's been pretty hyper and open this past week but funny too. He's been very well behaved and really doesn't get in much trouble unlike his siblings. Usually when I ask him to do something he says: "Ok Mamma, I will do it".

When I ask him if he needs to be changed (potty training is an ongoing process)
"Nope I'm fine" but the whole house reeks
Did you make the mess?
"Yes I did" ... well at least your honest... "Yes at least I'm honest".

He's so full of LIFE! Yes, how wonderful that he's feeling

Sunday May 9, 2010

This year Mother's Day was a tad less stress like compared to last. The sounds of my boys wishing me Happy Mother's Day was like a serenade.

Lennon who came home on Friday, so excited with a

plant, a necklace and a picture of him to give to me for Mother's Day. In light of it all, my oldest is graduating high school on the 22nd of May and turning 18, shortly after. YIKES! This is a big deal and I am glad that at this point is not being shadowed due to medical complications!

Monday May 24, 2010

Lennon's O2 was 100. It hadn't been that in a very long time. He gained weight and is now a whopping 51 lbs. Today we received some not so good news. We stopped the aspirin and added Vitamin K shots to help his bleeding and bruising. They checked his factor 5 and factor 7 levels, thinking and hoping that his blood is stable and that the liver is fine. However, levels are low and the liver is sick.

The ascites is back. The doctors couldn't drain it and he isn't a good candidate for a shunt. What does all this mean?

We don't have a choice but to move forward with another transplant evaluation.

My thoughts are jumbled and my heart aches. Lennon looks so good and is acting so healthy. It's hard to fathom that Lennon is ill and that once again we are facing another difficult journey…

Thursday June 10, 2010

There have been many questions to why Lennon needs another transplant. He is medically stable, and we don't need to rush.

Lennon has a clot in the portal vein. He has a thrombosis with the hepatic vein and a third clot was found in the vena cava. Due to the clots in the portal vein, the body created extra vessels to create pathways for blood flow, one of the reasons he looks like a map of waterways.

We also know that because his EBV levels are high, there is hepatitis in play and his liver will develop cirrhosis, which is a response to chronic damage to the liver. Add that the ultrasound showed enlarged organs, which is good and bad.

The chances of surviving a third liver transplant is about 30-40%. Lennon is at risk for some major blood loss and for the surgeons' to get through the scar tissue. The question with these odds is whether or not we should just live life and enjoy it while we can.

My heart his heavy.

Since we are talking about another transplants, we are

talking about being send to another hospital; perhaps one that is more specialized in pediatric organ transplants. We are moving forward with an evaluation, knowing that we could change our mind. The doctors need to write letters for insurance approval, and make a convincing case to another hospital. Lennon could be this way for 1-2 years before he would be too fragile for the surgery.

So much to consider and now we have to wait to be accepted.

I am trying to hold off on any medical decisions until the other hospital had a chance to look at Lennon's case

I still have a difficult time to wrap my head around this all. Be grateful do not take things for granted. Appreciate what we do have, dream for what we want without hate and judgment.

Honored and grateful to be his mom, to have my children, to be surrounded by people who love and care for us.
It is one day at a time – each day filled with love and appreciation.

Thursday June 24, 2010

7 years ago a little boy sneezed himself into the world. I firmly believe that with each child we learn something

new about love and life. I've learned to be the kind of mom that hopes to make decisions with their best interest in mind. It hasn't always been easy that parenting thing.

We are not throwing a huge party; instead we will have cake and watch a movie.

Sunday July 11, 2010

We are in Pittsburgh starting the journey of an evaluation. Lennon will give blood for the labs to do their testing. He will speak to the geneticist, psychologist and the liver transplant team. We will be here for a few days and then head home. Home so we can wait and find out if he will be listed.

Tuesday August 10, 2010

Lennon is on the transplant list for another liver. I have mixed emotions but really is there another choice?

If we do not move forward what kind of mom would I be to not save my son's life? I am glad they recommended the transplant rather than saying they can't do anything for him.

Allowing (probably not the right word) Lennon to die

doesn't seem to be an option, which is what would happen if we do nothing. The liver is already dying due to thrombosis and clotting. Allowing him to have a fighting chance is the right thing to do!

I will not knock what our local hospital has done because I truly belief that they have done everything possible. Kudos to them for doing what is best for Lennon and recommending that another hospital specialized in pediatric transplants may be better option.

The reality is that if I don't do anything and do not move forward I will feel guilty for not trying. By moving forward with another transplant I know that we have done everything in our power.

Thanks for your continuing prayers and positive thoughts.

Saturday August 21, 2010

It's pretty daunting the waiting game. My phone rang today and it was the hospital and my heart took an extra beat or two but talk about his blood oxygen. They checked the blood flow into his lungs and while it looked good, there is concern that his breathing is terribly increased.

One thing that we have gotten in place is transport to the hospital. Lennon and I will be flying from Charlottesville to Pittsburgh when the time comes. I wonder how he will do flying for about 3 hours. Will he be calm? Will he be stressed and freaked out?

Lennon is doing well however. He's enjoying school and just being normal. This past week he had homework and while he at first resisted the process, he was beaming with pride when he did it. He loves going to school. I think it's a combination of being around other kids and learning, being challenged a little.

Thursday September 2, 2010

Lennon had a bubble echo done due to low oxygen levels. His O2 changes from one minute to the next.

The capillaries cannot do what they need to do, which is referred to Arteriovenous Malformation (AVM), which is really just an abnormal collection of blood vessels.

Not good but I think something everyone thought this would be the case. The bubbles went into his heart within 3 heartbeats and according to the doctor it should take much longer than that if at all. One side of the heart was white and the next second so was the other side.

I called Pittsburgh and learned that this was the wrong test but instead of having be sedated again, they will use the results to help them assess Lennon for his number on the transplant list.

Lennon will move to the top of the list next week.

Sunday September 5, 2010

A hero is an ordinary individual who finds the strength to persevere and endure in spite of overwhelming obstacles.
Christopher Reeve

Some days I don't know how I manage. Today was one of those days. What I often don't write about is the cognitive disability that has impacted Lennon's life, his impulsiveness, inability to focus and/or listen, and inability to assess safety and risky situation and the lack of maturity for a 7 year old.
When you are with Lennon you are "on" all the time. I foster his independence but it comes with a price. He can't assess situations appropriately and jumping of the couch, well that is just fun. Or he will climb on the freezer to get himself a freezer pop just to run to me with scissors in hand.

I find myself wanting to tell Lennon that he can't do these things and then I push them aside, because he can do these things, because I encourage him to do these things.

Last night he unhooked his feeding tube, forget that I had to clean formula stains, Lennon indicated he is tired of the feeding tube. He tells me all the time he wants to start eating, and I remind him that until he does he will have to have the tube. He wants to be "normal" like the other kids in school.

Its not always like this. Lennon loves to share his love; he loves to show attention, sitting in the lap or lying on the couch with someone.

He is simply living in this world the best way he knows how, unconditionally. The stress remains the same and the frustration and the tiredness I feel by the time the day is over, knowing I will have to do it all over again tomorrow. And again, I look forward to every morning, because I know that during the day we will spend special loving moments together, hugging, cuddling on the couch, even if only for a minute.

I was looking for something tonight for inner strength and I came across the quote from Christopher Reeve. It lifted me and its own right made me acknowledge myself and the person I am in Lennon's life.

Monday October 11, 2010

I don't think Lennon knows anything else other than just be himself and live life. He doesn't know anything different. Lennon is affectionate sometimes too much. He reminds me I should always be who I am, love every day, get mad and get over it, be passionate about the people and things you love – even if they are just ideals and even if they don't conform with most people i.e. society.

This morning his gentleness, compassion and thoughtfulness that we are able to see on days he's feeling well shines. After his morning ritual of bath time and picking out his breakfast, he went to talk to his brother. When he returned he said:" Sorry it took so long, but I had to say hi to him". Never apologize for talking to the people you love. Lennon certainly lets everyone know that he thinks about him or her, that he loves him or her and that they matter to him.
Yesterday, he was looking through a magazine and saw a picture of a stick-figure family. "Hey mommy! This is us!" as he went on to recall everyone's name that matter to him. I love these moments. The moments that he clearly means: people I love you! Hear me! Listen to me! Pay attention to me!

In health news, Lennon's lungs are working less more and more. This transplant we are going ahead with is the only cure to save his life. We are waiting on the top of the list.

Tuesday November 9, 2010

A liver transplant anniversary should be a big celebration of life, his life. Clearly in my head I know that the past liver transplants have saved his life, and it is heavy in my heart that we will go through this again.

I remember the time when he came home like a wilted little flower who was unable to embrace life, which appeared depressed and the light in his eyes was gone. I remember the days and months it has taken for him to be Lennon. To be center stage, to be full of life, to be funny, to keep us on our toes, to be charming and even manipulating everyone around him to get his way. I remember the experiences in my heart and in my head.

I want to celebrate his chance of having a wonderful life. I worry about my kids how they are coping and how they will be coping.

It is a hard sitting at the edge every day and when the phone rings looking, wondering, hoping, dreading that its the hospital telling me that they have had an offer for a liver. My heart hurts reflecting on the experiences we have had already and the experience to come.

Wednesday November 17, 2010

Just talked to Pittsburgh and we are still. He will go up on the list again with 53 points. The scans we did with his lungs confirmed that Lennon has Hepatopulmonary Syndrome, A Liver-Induced Lung Vascular Disorder. Nothing changes with moving ahead with the transplant and we will hope that his lungs will hold out until it happens.

Lennon has learned to identify his name and write it too except if forgets the second n. He's making progress!

Wednesday December 1, 2010

Lennon is sick, so sick actually that he cannot participate in PE. As Lennon continues to be ill, he may need oxygen but it comes with an incredible risk. For some people in Lennon's situation, oxygen can make him loopy and change his personality.

It is so hard to watch your life loving boy run and his lips and fingers are turning blue, all because his lungs are not receiving enough oxygen.

Wednesday December 8, 2010

I am struggling to get into the spirit of the season and here is Lennon making Salt Dough Ornaments.

Live life with determination and fun.

Sunday December 26, 2010

We survived Christmas at home and Lennon's toes are tinted blue and his breathing is labored.

Santa got him a cleaning trolley with his own broom, mop, bucket, dustpan, spray bottle and a Diego Rescue Center. He loves both of them very much. He has already mopped the kitchen and rescued animals numerous times a day.

Thursday January 20th

The phone rang and it all appeared so familiar. We have a possible match; please make your way to Pittsburgh. ON the phone with Angel Flight we were expected at the airport at 3:30!

Our wonderful nurse almost received a speeding ticket. The moment we told the office, the reason for speeding, he let us go and told us to be safe.

Lennon and I waited at the airport. He was amazed at the planes flying in.

The four-seater Cessna took us into the air with a forecast of snow along the way. Lennon filled with excitement looked down onto the earth, asking a million questions about the fields down below. Arriving at a snow covered airport, an ambulance waited to zip us through the city of Steel.

Lennon went into the operating room at 2 a.m.

The doctor approached the waiting room with a serious look upon his face. Lennon is extremely critical because of major blood loss and connectivity issues and he is need of transfusions. The doctor told me they couldn't find the portal vein and so they are rerouting veins until they can move forward with the connectivity. The doctor's are struggling but are not giving up.

It's come down to this, a matter of life and death.

Happiness for doctors means 20% of liver function.

12 hours and counting and he's still in surgery.

YES, connections are happening, but they are not connecting the bile duct quite yet. Instead, they are going to allow him to rest with sedation on the breathing tube.

Lennon is not out of the woods. So pardon me if I am cautiously optimistic with a splash of hope. Lennon is on his way to the ICU.

The honesty of his doctors is refreshing. For folks who are trained and do this on quite a regular basis, this was one of the hardest, toughest and most difficult transplants he's ever encountered.

My boy is a true fighter, despite the blood-pressure drop and potential neurological concerns and the significant dangerously amount of blood loss, his heart, it never stopped. Not one a single beat.

There's a lot of technical stuff the doctors said that I wouldn't gross you out with. Lennon will go back into surgery next week to connect the bile duct. In the mean time, Lennon is going to ICU to recover from today to start the healing process. One reason they are waiting is to keep Lennon strong and make sure he can handle it. They feel that if they wait with the bile duct surgery. It will be better for Lennon due to the 15-hour marathon he just had in the OR.

I would like to tell you how I feel but the words elude me at this time. I am anxious to see him and let him know about all the prayers that were send for him, about him. Well ok you know what I mean. I am beyond exhausted and grateful to you all for being there/here with me in thought and prayer.

The liver IS WORKING!

AFTERWORD

Lennon is 11 years old at the time of this publishing. He has made a miraculous recovery from his last liver transplant in 2011. He is fully engaged in school and enjoys playing video games and is an avid reader. Despite his cognitive delays he continues to set an example of working hard and living life with determination.

You can continue to follow his journey on www.lennonsworld.com

ABOUT THE AUTHOR

Petra Monaco is a mother, author, artist and life coach. Petra's resilience in her early childhood years helped her hone the skills to maneuver the years of her youngest son's illness. In her book Lennon Steps, Petra talks about the early years and shared her experience and Lennon's journey through her blog Lennonsworld.com
Petra is an entrepreneur, visionary, dreamer and an inspiration to many as she continues to maneuver her world with Lennon's continued health needs as well as rearing her other children.
Petra's work can be found at www.fosterdlife.com she shares tips and tricks in how to cultivate your dreams to create an incredible life. She sells her artwork though www.hippiescreations.com continuing to create art that is soothing and healing to her heart.
Petra's twitter account is @petramonaco. She can also be found on her facebook pages for Petra Monaco and Hippie's Creations.

Made in the USA
Charleston, SC
03 February 2015